How to Make Decisions
with **Different Kinds** of
Student Assessment Data

How to Make Decisions
with **Different Kinds** of
Student Assessment Data

SUSAN M. BROOKHART

ASCD

Alexandria, Virginia USA

1703 N. Beauregard St. • Alexandria, VA 22311-1714 USA
Phone: 800-933-2723 or 703-578-9600 • Fax: 703-575-5400
Website: www.ascd.org • E-mail: member@ascd.org
Author guidelines: www.ascd.org/write

Deborah S. Delisle, *Executive Director;* Stefani Roth, *Publisher;* Genny Ostertag, *Director, Content Acquisitions;* Julie Houtz, *Director, Book Editing & Production;* Darcie Russell, *Senior Associate Editor;* Georgia Park, *Senior Graphic Designer;* Mike Kalyan, *Manager, Production Services;* Cynthia Stock, *Typesetter;* Kelly Marshall, *Senior Production Specialist*

All web links in this book are correct as of the publication date below but may have become inactive or otherwise modified since that time. If you notice a deactivated or changed link, please e-mail books@ascd.org with the words "Link Update" in the subject line. In your message, please specify the web link, the book title, and the page number on which the link appears.

PAPERBACK ISBN: 978-1-4166-2103-4   ASCD product #116003
PDF E-BOOK ISBN: 978-1-4166-2105-8; see Books in Print for other formats.
Quantity discounts: 10–49, 10%; 50+, 15%; 1,000+, special discounts (e-mail programteam@ascd.org or call 800-933-2723, ext. 5773, or 703-575-5773). For desk copies, go to www.ascd.org/deskcopy.

ASCD Member Book No. FY16-3. ASCD Member Books mail to Premium (P), Select (S), and Institutional Plus (I+) members on this schedule: Jan, PSI+; Feb, P; Apr, PSI+; May, P; Jul, PSI+; Aug, P; Sep, PSI+; Nov, PSI+; Dec, P. For current details on membership, see www.ascd.org/membership.

Library of Congress Cataloging-in-Publication Data

Names: Brookhart, Susan M.
Title: How to make decisions with different kinds of student assessment data
  / Susan M. Brookhart.
Description: Alexandria, Virginia : ASCD, 2015. | Includes bibliographical
  references and index.
Identifiers: LCCN 2015033290 | ISBN 9781416621034 (pbk.)
Subjects: LCSH: Educational tests and measurements—United States. | Grading
  and marking (Students)—United States. | Educational evaluation—United
  States.
Classification: LCC LB3051 .B7288 2015 | DDC 371.26--dc23 LC record available at
  http://lccn.loc.gov/2015033290

24 23 22 21 20 19 18 17 16   1 2 3 4 5 6 7 8 9 10

How to Make Decisions with Different Kinds of Student Assessment Data

Acknowledgments

The four-quadrant framework in this book has been in development for five years. I began the work at the invitation of Robert W. Lissitz, who asked me to present at the 2011 MARCES/MSDE (Maryland Assessment Research Center/ Maryland State Department of Education) conference *Informing the Practice of Teaching Using Formative and Interim Assessment: A Systems Approach* at the University of Maryland. I am grateful to him for posing the question of a systems approach, and I also thank the many people at that conference who encouraged me to develop the framework further. I am grateful to Margaret Heritage, who invited me to present this work at the Council of Chief State School Officers FAST SCASS (Formative Assessment for Students and Teachers State Collaborative on Assessment and Student Standards) in 2012, and to that organization for supporting further development of the framework. I am grateful to all the educators who have attended my assessment workshops and encouraged me to expand on the framework because they found it useful. This book is the result of their encouragement. I am grateful to my ASCD editors, Genny Ostertag and Darcie Russell: to Genny for believing this framework could be the basis for a book and to Darcie for editorial support. Of course, none of this work would have been possible without the love and support of my wonderful husband Frank and our daughters Carol and Rachel, to whom I am grateful for so much more than this book.

An Introduction to Different Kinds of Data

1

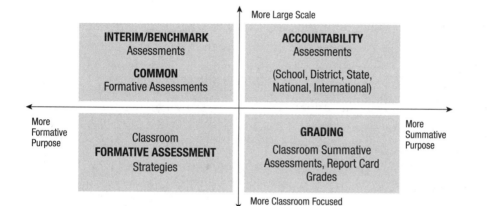

Simple logic does not always help us with data interpretation. Here are two examples, both of which are true stories.

Once during a workshop session, a school administrator explained to me that he saw standardized test scores as a sort of barometer. He aimed to make changes in his school that would lead to a rise in test scores, and that would be his indication that his reforms were successful. The analogy he gave me was the population of oysters in the Chesapeake Bay. Environmental reforms were needed in the bay area, changes were made, and the oyster numbers are increasing (see http://www.chesapeakebay.net/issues/issue/oysters for more information). Similarly, he explained, reforms in his school should lead to higher test scores.

The second example occurred at an airport, where I struck up a conversation with a businessman and his young son who were waiting for the same airport shuttle I was. The man said that he was really glad that his state now administered standardized tests, as per No Child Left Behind, because finally he had what he called a "bottom line" that he could watch to know how his child and his child's school were doing. His analogy was to the bottom line in a profit-and-loss statement in a business.

1

The administrator and the businessman dad were well-meaning people who valued education; they were not nay-sayers. They were both bright and successful individuals who applied logic and common sense to a problem they cared about. And they were both wrong.

Here's the thing. If you are an environmentalist or an oysterman, the oysters *are* the issue—or in the case of the Chesapeake Bay, one of the issues. Increasing the oyster population, to improve the habitat and the economy, *is* the purpose of the scientific reforms and management strategies. More oysters means the program is achieving its goal. Similarly, generating a profit *is* the purpose of being in business. Higher profits mean more money for shareholders, employees, and product development. Making money means your business is achieving its goal.

In contrast, raising test scores is not the purpose of education. The purpose of education has changed with society's needs and values over the years (Sloan, 2012). At this point in time, if you ask people the purpose of education, you will get answers such as these: to create adults who can compete in a global economy, to create informed citizens who can participate in the democratic process, to create critical thinkers and problem solvers, to create lifelong learners, or to create emotionally healthy adults who can engage in meaningful relationships. Obviously, no test score can tell you whether you have achieved these things.

The less obvious problem with our well-meaning administrator and businessman is that *even if you limit your interest to academic learning outcomes, raising test scores is not the purpose of education. The students' learning is.* Test scores are a measure of student learning, but they are not the thing itself. In our analogies, the oysters and the money were themselves the objects of interest. You can count oysters, and you can count money, but you can't "count" learning.

The best you can do to measure learning is to use a *mental measurement* that, if well designed, is a measure of learning in a limited domain. The key is to define clearly what that domain is, use a test or performance assessment that taps this domain in known ways, use a score scale with known properties that maps the student's performance back to the domain, and interpret that score scale correctly when making inferences about student learning. The purpose of this book is to explain just enough about the properties of data on student learning so that you can make those inferences well. Then—and only then—can you make sound decisions. Another name for this purpose is *developing assessment literacy*. As the examples demonstrate, literacy in educational assessment involves more than counting or ranking. It involves specifying *what specific learning* you are measuring; understanding how the questions or tasks in the measure form a sample of that domain of learning; understanding properties of the scales, numbers, or categories used in the measurement; and being able to reason from all these things to make sound interpretations and decisions.

To complicate matters a bit, as the title of this book indicates, there are different kinds of data. For most educational decisions, you will want to mix the different kinds of data to broaden and deepen the pool of information about student learning that you use to monitor and improve that learning. You will want to know which kinds of data to watch, and when, in order to evaluate the effectiveness of your decisions. This book will help you do that in two ways. First, it offers a framework for thinking about assessment systems that categorizes different measures of student learning. Understanding how information differs from one category to another will help you interpret data. Second, this book offers some insights into different types of scores. Understanding different types of scores and their meanings will help you interpret data properly, as well. Equipped with an understanding of these two big ideas, your data interpretation and subsequent decisions will be more sound, more valid, and more useful.

The Purposes and Uses of Data

The phrase "data-based decision making" is used often and has many meanings. Teachers use data to answer questions about students. Groups of teachers and building administrators use data to answer questions about students, classes, programs, and their school. Central office administrators use data to make decisions about teachers, as well as students, classes, programs, and schools. An Internet search on "data-based decision making" will bring up dozens of PowerPoint presentations, PDFs, images, and plans. Many books also address this theme.

It may seem like an obvious point, but the data you choose should be related to the intended purpose. If I want to make a tablecloth, I need to measure the length and width of the table; measuring its height won't help me much. The same principle operates in making decisions about student learning, but it's less easy to see. For example, if I want to make a decision about which reading skills to emphasize in my reading class, shouldn't I just look up students' scores on the state reading test? No. What the state reading test measures is general, overall "reading achievement," as defined by a whole set of reading standards. State test results will give you a sense of how your students do at "reading in general," as defined by whatever reading standards your state says its test measures, taken all together.

For example, the Smarter Balanced Assessment Consortium says that, regarding reading, its assessments can support this claim: "Students can read closely and analytically to comprehend a range of increasingly complex literary and informational texts" (Smarter Balanced, 2014). If I'm a teacher with a student whose assessment results suggest he can't do that very well, how do I design instruction for him? Low test results relative to this claim suggest a general decision—more or different reading instruction—but don't provide any clues about what aspects of reading to emphasize, remediate, or build on. To design reading instruction for that student, I'll need different data, assessment data that give a more fine-grained description of what the student can and cannot do as he reads.

In this simple example, reasoning from data is a two-step process. Data from the standardized accountability assessment help me identify a problem (Arland doesn't read proficiently) and lead me to another question: Why? To answer that second question, I need different data, because the reading accountability test doesn't give me information that is specific enough. Using complementary kinds of data for educational problem solving requires understanding different kinds of data.

This focus on a deeper understanding of data about student learning is what sets this book apart from other data books. I will, of course, also talk about how to use the data to inform instructional improvement. Two other excellent books that talk about using data to inform instructional improvement are *Data Wise* by Boudett, City, and Murnane (2013) and *Using Data to Focus Instructional Improvement* by James-Ward, Fisher, Frey, and Lapp (2013).

This book complements those and other books about data by focusing on developing a clearer understanding of exactly what test scores and other data about student learning *are* and what they *mean*. As an analogy, think about reading a Shakespeare play in a high school English class. If you read the play with a basic understanding of the English language, you will understand the plot. If you take the time to learn some Shakespearean vocabulary, you will understand the plot and the word-play nuances that unlock some of the humor and characterization in the play. In other words, you will understand the play better. Similarly, if you do data-based decision making with a basic understanding of assessment and of numbers, you will be able to make general decisions. If you learn some concepts about how educational assessments are constructed and some nuances about what their results mean, you will understand better what the data are telling you about your students' achievement.

Data About Student Learning

One way to organize and describe the different kinds of data about student learning is to use a four-quadrant framework (Brookhart, 2013). This framework allows us to group different kinds of data according to general type and purpose and to examine how they complement each other. It gives us some vocabulary to describe "assessment" in more specific terms. Figure 1.1 shows a four-quadrant framework for describing different kinds of assessments of student learning. The framework does not attempt to cover other data of interest to educators (e.g., student attendance, the number of books in the library, the ratio of students to teachers), just assessments of student learning.

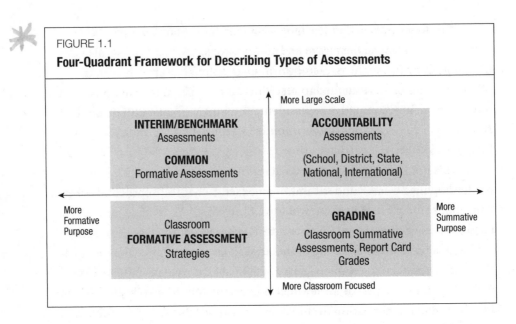

FIGURE 1.1

Four-Quadrant Framework for Describing Types of Assessments

This framework will help you use different types of data to get richer, fuller information for your classroom decisions. The response of teachers and administrators to this framework has been quite positive. I have found that people are looking for a way to describe their "assessment system" that is more than just a long list of assessments.

Two dimensions: Purpose and focus

The framework in Figure 1.1 defines two dimensions on which assessment of student learning can be described: intended *purpose* for the information (formative or summative) and intended *focus* of the information (classroom or large scale). Of course, individual students are the ones who are assessed in all cases; even the large-scale state accountability test is administered to individual students. The focus dimension is about the place where the information is centered, and for large-scale assessments that focus is across individuals, classrooms, and schools.

Purpose. If learning is the main emphasis in education, then the distinction in purpose—between assessment that informs learning and assessment that certifies that learning—is important. Many readers will be familiar with balancing formative and summative assessment in their classroom practice. Formative assessment, or assessment *for* learning, occurs during learning and is intended to result in improved learning (Moss & Brookhart, 2009). Summative assessment, or assessment *of* learning, occurs after an episode of learning and is intended to summarize the student's achievement level at a particular time (Moss, 2013). Typically, formative assessment items and tasks, and formative feedback, tackle next-step-sized learning targets. By the time summative assessment is appropriate, the outcome may be broader. As a somewhat oversimplified illustration, feedback on a 2nd grader's writing might be about capitalization and punctuation today and ideas tomorrow, and the final graded writing sample may appraise both.

Focus. The location of reference for the learning information is the other dimension—whether assessment is centered in the classroom or in a large-scale context. Some readers may be less familiar with distinguishing classroom-focused from large-scale assessments than they are with distinguishing formative and summative assessment purposes. After all, it's students in classrooms who take all the assessments, right? In Chapters 2 through 5, you will see that it is very useful to distinguish assessments that are primarily focused on the learning that occurs in one classroom, with its particular instructional context, from assessments that are primarily focused on generalizing across classroom contexts. The two differ in important ways, most notably on what specific learning is assessed and in the kinds of numbers that are used to quantify student performance. Some of that assessment information is meant for classroom use, and some is meant to be aggregated across classrooms for larger-scale evaluation—of a course, a program, or a school, for example.

Four quadrants

Crossing the two dimensions results in four quadrants that define the four major types of assessment of student learning that are used in schools, or what I have been calling "different kinds of data." These types are formative classroom assessment; interim/benchmark assessment, including "common formative assessments" that are intended to be given in more than one classroom; summative (graded) classroom assessment; and summative (accountability) large-scale assessment. I'll briefly describe each type here and then devote a chapter to each.

Formative assessment: Formative purpose, classroom focus. Formative assessment is an active and intentional learning process that partners teachers and students to continuously and systematically gather evidence of learning with the express goal of improving student achievement (definition from Moss & Brookhart, 2009, p. 6; also see Wiliam, 2010). Formative assessment involves strategies such as the following (Moss & Brookhart, 2009; Wiliam, 2010):

- Sharing learning targets and criteria for success with students
- Feedback that feeds forward, from teachers, peers, or other sources
- Student self-assessment and goal setting
- Using strategic questions and engaging students in asking effective questions

One of the hallmarks of formative classroom assessment is student involvement. Formative assessment strategies aim to develop assessment-capable students who can see where they are headed (they can envision a learning target and know what it represents), take stock of where they are in relation to the target, and understand what they need to do next to continue to approach the learning target. Formative assessment's foundation is the students' clear concept of a learning target, or even a broader learning goal, and a clear understanding of what achievement of that goal looks like. This means students understand the criteria for success, or what Moss and I call "student look-fors" (Moss & Brookhart, 2009). Receiving feedback and using it to improve, setting goals and monitoring progress toward them, and asking effective questions all are based on the foundation of understanding "what I am trying to learn."

In recent years, people have quibbled over whether students have to be involved in making decisions about assessment results in order for the assessment to be formative. One of the reasons for the confusion is ignoring the distinction between classroom-focused and large-scale assessment. Students have to be involved in *classroom* formative assessment, which works only when students take action on what they should do next in their learning. They can't take effective cognitive action if they aren't involved in making the decisions. However, students don't necessarily have to be involved in decisions made about large-scale assessments that are intended to be formative in purpose. Teachers may use these results to modify instruction, for example, without the students knowing about it.

I have found that the focus dimension—classroom versus large scale—helps enormously with the vocabulary problem educators have been struggling with regarding formative assessment. For example, I was talking with a principal who thought "formative assessment" had to refer to the interim assessments his district purchased from a testing company, and so he didn't know what to make of the formative assessment strategies that occur within daily lessons—which was the topic I was at his school to address. I showed him the four-quadrant framework, and he found it immediately helpful. We might not be able to do much about the fact that the term *formative assessment* is currently used in too many different ways, but we certainly can make sure that we understand exactly what we are talking about for any specific data and interpret the data accordingly. This framework will help you do that.

Interim assessment: Formative purpose, large-scale focus. Teachers can use interim/benchmark assessments that do not involve students—other than to respond to assessment items or tasks—to inform instructional planning for those students or even for future students. This is a formative purpose, although it's not what I generally have in mind when I use the term *formative assessment*; to me, that term usually means classroom formative assessment. Interim assessment and classroom formative assessment are different from each other in a couple of ways. One difference is that interim assessment data can be aggregated, whereas classroom formative assessment data cannot. The second difference is that the users of interim assessment data are teachers, whereas the users of formative assessment data are students and teachers. The four-quadrant framework makes these differences explicit, because interim assessment is in the "large-scale" space, above the axis, and formative classroom assessment is in the "classroom-focused" space, below the axis. In Chapters 3 and 5 I'll say more about what this means for interpreting and using assessment results.

There is a place for assessment information that can inform future instructional decisions and even administrative decisions. An example might be using interim assessments three times a year, each to inform planning of the next nine weeks of mathematics instruction, or combining information from several interim assessments to decide that, given limited funds, the school will hire a mathematics specialist next year instead of another classroom teacher. Some schools use assessments they call "common formative assessments," which they administer in more than one class, typically across a grade level and a subject area. If common formative assessments are used for planning (and not grading), they fit in this category.

Some interim/benchmark assessments or common formative assessments are also used for classroom grading or other evaluative purposes (Abrams & McMillan, 2013). This is not a recommended practice, and the four-quadrant framework helps us see why. Using data for several different purposes at once *is* possible, but it requires making sure that the data are valid for both purposes. Validating data for two different uses is very difficult to do, and the interaction of the different uses usually ends up changing the meaning of assessment results for both purposes (Koch & DeLuca, 2012). I'll have more to say about this in Chapter 5, as well.

Interim/benchmark assessment and common formative assessment involve practices such as the following:

- Using an item bank to construct tests at checkpoint times—for example, at the end of a unit or quarterly, for all students taking a certain subject in a certain grade
- Using teacher-made tests, and sometimes performance assessments, at checkpoint times—for example, at the end of a unit or quarterly, for all students taking a certain subject in a certain grade
- Using commercially published tests at checkpoint times
- Using curriculum-based progress-monitoring data

Grading: Summative purpose, classroom focus. Classroom grading comes in two forms: (1) individual grades—summative assessment via tests or performance assessments or any other graded assignments, and (2) report card grades (Brookhart, 2011). A report card grade is dependent on the quality of the information in the individual assignments on which it is based. Great procedures for report card summarizing cannot make up for poor-quality assessment information. On the other hand, high-quality assessment information, summarized poorly, does not produce a meaningful report card grade either. Both high-quality component information and summarizing methods that preserve intended meaning in the composite are necessary.

Classroom grades are a longstanding tradition in education and have been the subject of controversy for years (Brookhart, in press). Classroom grades typically report on unit-sized (or thereabouts) "chunks" of classroom learning. Classroom grades are typically expressed either as percentages or on short scales made up of achievement categories (e.g., *ABCDF* or Advanced, Proficient, Basic, Below Basic). Chapter 4 will discuss these points in more detail.

Large-scale accountability assessment: Summative purpose, large-scale focus. Finally, there is summative, large-scale accountability assessment. State tests fit here, as well as national and international comparison studies. Large-scale accountability assessment has been the subject of much interest and study recently (Perie, Park, & Klau, 2007), so I don't have to defend its place in the framework. Many educators realize the potential value of large-scale accountability tests but feel they may have more influence than they should (Shepard, 2000). Chapter 2 will describe how accountability tests typically furnish data about learning at a very large grain size (e.g., reading, mathematics) and explain how to interpret data that may be norm-referenced, criterion-referenced, or "standards-referenced," which draws a bit from both (Brookhart & Nitko, 2015).

Balanced Assessment

Looking at the framework, you might think that a balanced assessment system should simply contain equal amounts of assessment from each of the four quadrants. This is not true.

Some materials designed for state and local administrators suggest that a balanced assessment system should be based on a tiered or pyramid-style model (e.g., Crane, 2010; Perie, Marion, & Gong, 2009). Classroom assessment, the bottom portion of the pyramid, is the most common or frequent kind of assessment, followed by interim assessment and then state accountability assessment. This pyramid model lumps all classroom assessment together and misses the opportunity to specify a good balance between classroom formative assessment and classroom summative assessment.

The four-quadrant framework privileges classroom-level data by devoting a dimension—and therefore half of the framework—to it. The classroom is the place where learning happens, and if we ignore the information closest to the learning, we lose a lot of fine-grained and diagnostic information. I argue for an assessment balance that looks more like Figure 1.2.

FIGURE 1.2

Achieving Balance in an Assessment System

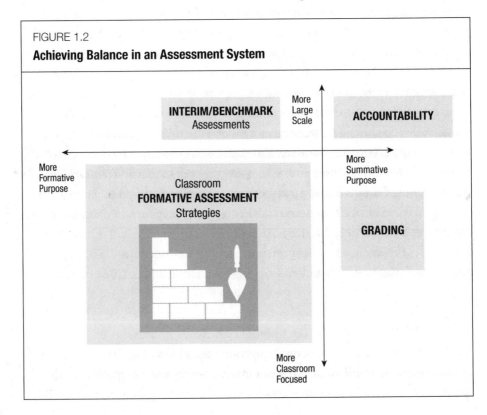

Classroom formative assessment is the assessment that is best positioned to help improve learning. Well-designed classroom formative assessment focuses information on the growing edge of learning, puts the information in the hands of the students, and supports small, incremental, and immediate next steps in learning (Andrade, 2010; Black & Wiliam, 1998; Datnow & Hubbard, 2015; Moss & Brookhart, 2009). That's why Figure 1.2 enlarges the classroom formative assessment quadrant and suggests that this quadrant is the foundation of a balanced assessment system.

All types of assessment have a place, however. It is when data are used without an understanding of what they are *for* (e.g., a high school decides to use data from its benchmark assessment as part of students' report card grades to "make them take it seriously") that we get into trouble. I wrote this book to support informed use of the different kinds of data and to discourage using data for purposes for which the data are not suited.

How Sound Is Your Information?

The suitability of assessment results for particular purposes has a name: *validity*. This concept is central to educational assessment. Remember the businessman's bottom line? Because making money *is* a goal of his business, the amount of money made is one valid measure of the success of the business. Of course, it's not the only measure, because the business may have other goals, but clearly the bottom line is an important measure.

Contrast this with assessments that measure student learning. We can't directly measure that. We can't get "inside a kid's head." So we use "mental measures" that we construct according to sets of rules that we think might give us good estimates of student learning. Occasionally the set of rules is something like this: "Select a correct answer for each of these test items; for each answer you select, you will get one point; your score will be your total number of points divided by the number of possible points."

You can see there are several questions that need to be asked before we can be confident about what the score means. Some of those questions are about the test items. How much confidence you have that the score is a valid measure of what you want to know depends on the answers to questions such as these:

- What were those test questions about? Were they about things the students had an opportunity to learn? Were they a representative mix of all the things the students were supposed to learn about the topic—that is, of all the possible questions you could have asked, how representative a sample is the set of questions you actually asked?
- Were the questions well written and clear? Were they at an appropriate level of difficulty? Did students understand all the words in the questions?
- Did students need any other specialized knowledge to answer the questions, besides what the questions were trying to test (e.g., did students need background knowledge on anything in a scenario, such as in a word problem or a reading passage), that might affect the test question's ability to measure achievement?
- Did the questions ask students to use thinking skills in the manner your learning outcomes intended (e.g., were students supposed to just recall information, or were they supposed to be able to use information to solve a problem or analyze a situation)?

Some of those questions are about the scoring procedure. How much confidence you have that the score is a valid measure of what you want to know also depends on the answers to questions such as these:

- Does each of those one-point questions really contribute about the same value or weight to the total score? Should some questions be worth more than others—and if so, why?
- Are there enough questions to ensure that the results provide you with an accurate sense of what students know and not just an indicator of chance performance? Are there enough questions to reasonably support using the percentage scale you have chosen (e.g., if there are only two questions, the only possible scores are 0, 50, and 100, which is a little silly).

This is not an exhaustive list of questions, but it should be enough to show you how you need to build a bridge of reasoning and evidence between the score on any assessment and its meaning in a way that is not necessary for concrete measures like number of oysters or amount of money. This list of questions should also show you that the validity questions will differ for different kinds of data. Finally, the list should illustrate that behind questions about the meaning of a measure and its suitability for its purpose (validity), there are also some questions about the accuracy and consistency of the measure (reliability). You can't make meaningful decisions if you have inaccurate data.

As I describe the different kinds of data in Chapters 2 through 5, I'll try to highlight particular validity and reliability issues that are especially important for common uses of each kind of data. This book is not meant to be a substitute for a more thorough treatment of educational measurement (Brookhart & Nitko, 2015), but rather to be a guide to those who use data in practical ways in schools. To show that validity is important for everyone who uses educational data, not just for measurement experts, I ask you to consider two current examples that have validity questions at their core.

The issue of using large-scale, standardized tests as measures of school accountability with associated consequences has been with us for a while but became particularly salient when the No Child Left Behind Act was signed in 2002 (NCLB, 2002). Arguments about the suitability of large-scale tests to measure the quality of schooling range on both sides of the issue, and they hinge on validity questions. What do those tests measure? Are they the right indicators for the purpose of judging school quality? Are there other indicators that should be considered? Are the resulting judgments about school quality accurate?

Another current issue with validity questions at its core is the use of student assessment results as part of teacher evaluation systems (ISBE, 2013; NYSED, 2014). Arguments about the suitability of assessments for this purpose also range on both sides of the issue, and they too hinge on validity questions. What assessments are most appropriate for any given teacher, subject, or grade level? Is the student achievement thus measured really a measure of teacher quality? Do various statistical treatments applied to scores (e.g., pre-post gains, value-added models) appropriately remove the effects of irrelevant information and leave relevant information in the results? Are the resulting conclusions about teacher quality accurate?

Although these are hot-button issues, I believe that similar issues at the classroom level are equally important. Does your classroom assessment actually give you the information you think it does and support your next instructional move? Does your classroom assessment give your student an accurate picture of exactly what she needs to focus on next in order to improve in the way that she wants to? It always angers me that people say that daily classroom decisions are "less important" in some way than, say, medical decisions. Although it's true that poor medical decisions can lead to death, I always say that "messing with a kid's mind" has an equally dire consequence. I realize that an unintended wrong turn in instruction might last five minutes and can be corrected in the next five minutes, but I submit that it risks confusing the student or, at a minimum, wasting five minutes of precious learning time. We need to champion the cause of high-quality data for classroom use as well as large-scale uses, even though such data won't make headlines.

The Organization of This Book

Each of the next four chapters treats one quadrant of the framework. The chapter begins with a definition and a description of the kind or kinds of data available in that quadrant. I describe what you can (and can't) learn from these kinds of data, which in turn is based on the kind of learning and the grain size of the constructs that are commonly measured by that kind of data. Each chapter explains how to interpret common kinds of scores usually associated with that kind of data. Of course, I provide examples in each chapter.

In the process, I hope to demystify some quantitative concepts—not only different kinds of scores (e.g., what's the difference between a percentile rank and a percentage?), but also some principles (e.g., how aggregation can mask patterns in data, the difference between norm referencing and criterion referencing) and issues (e.g., the issues involved in measuring student growth, how to decide whether data are comparable—the "apples and oranges" issue). However, this is not a mathematics or statistics book. It is an "explaining" book. Just as you learned to read words, you can learn to "read" numbers.

Some words mean different things in different contexts. It may surprise you to learn the same is true for numbers.

The book concludes with three additional chapters. Chapter 6 discusses how to combine the different kinds of data about student learning, plus additional data about instruction, school culture, and resources, to answer questions about student learning and make decisions about what to do. Chapter 7 explains how to use different kinds of data about student learning to evaluate those decisions. Chapter 8 brings us back to the purpose of this book—to make you a better "reader" of data, who can reason with assessment results to arrive at defensible, effective decisions.

2 | Large-Scale Accountability Assessments

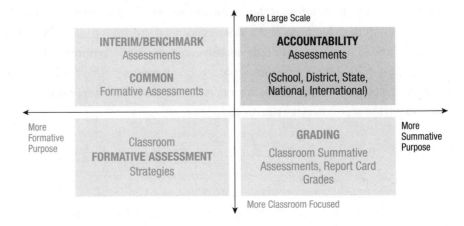

More Large Scale

| INTERIM/BENCHMARK Assessments | ACCOUNTABILITY Assessments |
| COMMON Formative Assessments | (School, District, State, National, International) |

More Formative Purpose

Classroom **FORMATIVE ASSESSMENT** Strategies

GRADING Classroom Summative Assessments, Report Card Grades

More Summative Purpose

More Classroom Focused

Large-scale accountability assessments are summative assessments because they report student achievement at a particular point in time and because schools, districts, and states are judged according to their results. Changes might be made based on those results—illustrating the fluidity between "summative" and "formative"—but at that point in time, evaluative judgments are made.

States mandate the use of particular assessments as part of their compliance with the No Child Left Behind law (2002). In recent years, the advent of the Common Core State Standards triggered the formation of two consortia to create assessments: the Partnership for Assessment of Readiness for College and Careers (PARCC, www.parcconline.org) and the Smarter Balanced Assessment Consortium (www.smarterbalanced.org). In addition, two consortia are working on alternative assessments for the Common Core State Standards: the National Center and State Collaborative (NCSC, www.ncscpartners.org) and the Dynamic Learning Maps Alternate Assessment System consortium (DLM, www.dynamiclearningmaps.org).

There are other large-scale assessments of student achievement besides state tests. The National Assessment of Educational Progress (NAEP, nces.ed.gov/nationsreportcard/) measures what students in the United States know and can do. The results are used for research and public information, and they lead to some accountability at the state level, as state-level results can be used to compare performances of students in different states and to evaluate the rigor of different states' accountability tests (Bandeira de Mello, Blankenship, & McLaughlin, 2009). Because of its broad scope, NAEP makes extensive use of sampling. Students are sampled, and even the items and tasks that students do are sampled. Scores are put together to make state and national reports, but because no one student took the whole NAEP assessment, there is no way to get an individual score.

High school graduation tests are a special case in this large-scale accountability quadrant because they are reported not only in the aggregate but also as individual results with serious consequences (McIntosh, 2012). If high school graduation tests were plotted as a point in this quadrant, they would be near the bottom, close to the classroom-focused assessments.

Types of Data Available

Large-scale accountability assessments give the largest grain-size information of all of the kinds of assessment in our four quadrants. For example, a school result may be that 58 percent of its students in grade 8 are proficient in reading. This is a piece of data, for sure, but it's very general—summarizing across all the students in grade 8 in a school and all the aspects of reading the assessment measured. And if you think about it, there will be other aspects of reading that were not assessed. The general public will interpret "58 percent of students proficient in the aspects of reading that were assessed" to mean "58 percent of students proficient in everything we could possibly want to assess about reading." Actually, if the test is well designed, this interpretation may even be justified, but with each "bigger" interpretation you lose some certainty about your conclusions.

Large-grain-size results are more useful for policy decisions than for instructional decisions. Some large-scale tests acknowledge this fact explicitly (e.g., Smarter Balanced 2013a, 2013b). However, what starts as a policy decision can quickly begin to feel like instructional mandates, as policies begin to affect schools (Au, 2007). Of course, you have to pay attention to something as important as large-scale accountability assessments. But it's important to keep in mind what they do and don't measure. Pronouncements about the performance of large groups of students in broad areas (e.g., reading, mathematics, science) raise more questions than they answer and should send you scurrying for smaller-grained information—again mostly at the classroom level. Large-scale results give you some clues about which areas to look in and what to look for. Don't be tempted to draw conclusions from them (e.g., "Our students need to read more" or "We need to alter our reading instruction"). Such conclusions are *not* warranted from large-scale data.

Large-scale results set up a problem to solve. Part of the solution strategy will be to search for more data in logical places. For example, you might seek classroom-level information about student achievement in the general domain. You also might look at the available resources, including both time and materials, in that domain, the expertise and instructional repertoire of the teachers who teach in that domain, and students' relevant background and experiences, including prior educational experiences, in that domain. Finally, you put this all together into a tentative conclusion and make an action plan that includes evaluating whether your plan leads to expected improvements.

Domain assessed

Large-scale accountability assessments most often assess achievement in broad domains such as reading, mathematics, and science. Assessments are built to state standards, but they may have only a few items or tasks representing any given standard. Therefore, they don't report achievement at the level of an individual standard, but rather report at the level of the subject-area domain. This matches their purpose. As mentioned earlier, large-scale accountability assessments are mostly for the purpose of informing policy decisions about schools.

For that purpose, knowing the percentage of students who are proficient in reading, for example, is useful information. More fine-grained information about specific strengths and weaknesses in reading is more useful for instructional decisions—decisions about what and how to teach students—rather than policy decisions about personnel or curriculum. Schools that do use large-scale accountability tests as part of data-driven decision making use the large-scale results to frame questions.

For example, large-scale accountability results might cause a district to ask, "Why are our special education students doing better in mathematics than in reading?" or "Why has our percentage of proficient readers increased over the last three years, while our percentage of students proficient in mathematics has stayed the same?" To answer those questions, you need information about student achievement and about instruction at the classroom level.

Methods and results

This chapter focuses on the test development process and proficiency-level categories. I also discuss scale scores, because they form the scale on which the cut scores for proficiency-level categories are determined. For this chapter, it's enough to know that scale scores are a measuring scale for the amount of achievement represented by students' performance on accountability tests. More detail about scale scores, norms, and percentile ranks, which are common metrics for presenting large-scale assessment results, is included in the next chapter. There is a certain amount of overlap in scoring information for all large-scale assessments, both accountability tests and interim/benchmark assessments. I have divided the information according to the quadrant in which it will be most useful for our discussion.

Most large-scale assessments follow a development process like the one diagrammed in Figure 2.1, which summarizes the process. The test development process includes more details at each step, and not every assessment will follow all of these steps in this exact order. Nevertheless, I think it's useful to see just "how the sausage is made" in order to understand the results.

The first step in developing a large-scale accountability assessment is to prepare an overall plan. This step should start with analyzing the domain of learning to be assessed—for example, mathematics. What exactly does "mathematics" mean in the intended assessment? The domain is then modeled, by asking—and acting upon—a series of questions. What claims will be made about

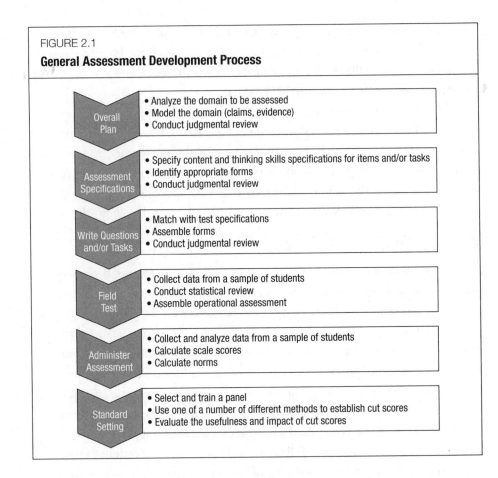

FIGURE 2.1
General Assessment Development Process

Overall Plan
- Analyze the domain to be assessed
- Model the domain (claims, evidence)
- Conduct judgmental review

Assessment Specifications
- Specify content and thinking skills specifications for items and/or tasks
- Identify appropriate forms
- Conduct judgmental review

Write Questions and/or Tasks
- Match with test specifications
- Assemble forms
- Conduct judgmental review

Field Test
- Collect data from a sample of students
- Conduct statistical review
- Assemble operational assessment

Administer Assessment
- Collect and analyze data from a sample of students
- Calculate scale scores
- Calculate norms

Standard Setting
- Select and train a panel
- Use one of a number of different methods to establish cut scores
- Evaluate the usefulness and impact of cut scores

students' achievement in mathematics? For state assessments, these claims necessarily relate to the state standards. What evidence is needed to support this kind of claim? What sorts of things will students need to show they can do at various levels of achievement? Often, the answers to these questions are written into achievement level descriptors (ALDs) that describe student performance at different achievement levels (Huff, Steinberg, & Matts, 2010). The end result of this step is a conceptual plan for an assessment, which will then be put into operation as test specifications (sometimes called a "test blueprint"). Before moving to that step, assessment development experts and content experts evaluate the domain model, claims, and evidence, revising if necessary.

The second step in developing a large-scale accountability assessment is preparing the assessment specifications. How many of what kind of item, tapping exactly what content and thinking skills, are required? For tests with more than one form, the specifications also describe how each form will be built to ensure comparability. This step comes before writing the items or tasks; writing them then becomes "filling the prescription" in the assessment specifications (e.g., the assessment developer may need three items testing literal comprehension of 3rd-grade-level informational text). Again, experts review the specifications to make sure they match with the overall plan for the assessment.

Next, items or tasks are written and assembled into test forms according to the specifications. This time, experts review the assessment itself—and they know what they *think* it assesses. What the actual results of the assessment will be, however, is an empirical question. A sample of students is selected to field-test the assessment. For a brand-new assessment, this requires a pilot test. With ongoing assessments from assessment programs already in progress, field-test items are often sprinkled into operational assessments. After students take the assessment, their performance is analyzed statistically to make sure the items and tasks are performing as intended. Are any items too hard? Too easy? Are there any items in which student answer patterns seem unexpected? For example, if low-achieving students get a question correct that many higher-achieving students miss, the question will need to be revised. How are the items or tasks related to one another? Are there any items or tasks that don't seem to fit with the others? After all of this statistical review, items or tasks are retained, revised, or eliminated and organized into operational forms—the assessments as they will actually be used in live testing.

The assessment is administered to the appropriate sample, which for a state test is, of course, all students in the appropriate grade level except for those taking alternative assessments. For other large-scale tests, this is the point at which a nationally representative sample is sought in order to calculate norms for the test. Students' results are scaled using one of a number of methods. All scaling methods use an underlying psychometric theory to map students' responses to items or tasks onto a performance scale. This is an important point, so don't let your eyes glaze over because statistics are involved. The important point is conceptual: Scales *represent* student performance in order to measure it. They do not just "count" student performance in the sense of adding up "number of points earned." The meaning of student performance as measured by a scale depends on the scaling method used, but all scaling methods add additional information to what the scale score reports about a student's achievement. The simplest scales add information about where the student's performance is located with respect to other students' performance. More complex scaling methods add information about characteristics of the items or tasks, as well—for instance, how difficult they are or how well they discriminate among students. That additional information means that *when you are looking at a scale score for one of your students, you are looking at more than his performance.* You are looking at his performance *in light of some other information.*

Finally, for large-scale accountability assessments that need to report categories of achievement, "standard setting" must be done. "Standard" in this sense means cut score, not a state standard or a Common Core State Standard. There are several different methods for conducting a standard setting (Cizek, 2001). For our purposes, the important thing to know is that all standard-setting methods involve judgment. An expert panel, usually including teachers, is convened and trained on whatever method is to be used. Some of the methods judge students, other methods judge items, and some judge student work. Most of the methods are iterative: they set tentative cut scores, discuss them (often using data from the test results), and refine them. The goal is to decide where along the score scale the cuts should be made for whatever achievement categories are desired: Basic, Proficient, and Advanced, for example, or perhaps one cut score between Proficient and Not Proficient. Different standard-setting methods lead to different cut scores. Using data from the test administration, standard-setting panels can see and evaluate impact data, which illustrate the results of using particular cut scores. For example, a panel might see that using the cut scores it suggested, 50 percent of the students would be classified as Not Proficient and 50 percent would be classified as Proficient. If the panel members think it is unlikely that half of the students in a state would be Not Proficient, they might decide to lower the cut score. This description of the standard-setting process shows why "standards-referenced" assessment has some characteristics of norm-referenced assessment (because it begins with scale scores) and some characteristics of criterion-referenced assessment (because it involves judging performance against standards).

The PARCC and Smarter Balanced assessment consortia will be doing standard setting soon. At the time of this writing, both consortia had published performance-level descriptions for five (PARCC) or four (Smarter Balanced) levels of achievement. Their standard-setting studies will involve deciding on cut scores to map performance on their assessments onto the descriptions they have written.

PARCC. PARCC (2013) has chosen to report five levels of achievement on their English Language Arts/Literacy and Mathematics assessments. PARCC planned to conduct standard setting—identification of cut scores for these levels—in summer 2015. They have written Policy-Level PLDs (Performance Level Descriptors) and General Content PLDs. They will also write grade- and subject-specific PLDs to describe performance in specific grades and content areas.

Policy-Level PLDs describe educational implications for students at a particular performance level. In grade 11, students' achievement levels will be used to make college- and career-ready determinations. In grades 9 and 10, students' achievement levels will be used to determine whether students are on track (PARCC, 2013, p. 6) to be college- and career-ready. In grades 3 through 8, students' achievement levels will be used to determine whether they are prepared to engage in successful further study in a content area. For example, the policy claim for Level 5 performance on the PARCC ELA/Literacy assessment reads as follows:

> Students performing at this level demonstrate a distinguished command of the knowledge, skills, and practices embodied by the Common Core State Standards for English language arts/literacy assessed at grade 11. They are academically well prepared to engage successfully in entry-level, credit-bearing courses in College English Composition, Literature, and technical courses requiring college-level reading and writing. Students performing at this level are exempt

from having to take and pass placement tests in two- and four-year public institutions of higher education designed to determine whether they are academically prepared for such courses without need for remediation. (PARCC, 2013, p. 6)

General Content PLDs are written for the same five levels of achievement, but instead of describing the educational implications of students' performance, they describe what students know and can do. For example, the general content claim for Level 3 (of five levels) performance on the PARCC mathematics assessment reads as follows:

In mathematics, students at this level demonstrate the following as appropriate for the grade level at which they are assessed:

- Adequately solve some problems correctly involving the major content for their grade with connection to the Standards for Mathematical Practice;
- Adequately solve some problems correctly involving the additional and supporting content for their grade with connection to the Standards for Mathematical Practice;
- Adequately express grade level appropriate mathematical reasoning by constructing viable arguments, critiquing the reasoning of others and/or attending to precision when making mathematical statements;
- Adequately solve some real world problems correctly, showing some evidence of engaging in the Modeling practice; and
- Adequate fluency as set forth in the Standards for Mathematical Content in their grade. (PARCC, 2013, p. 11)

The phrasing for the grade-level and content-area PLDs will be similar to that used for the General Content PLDs, except that references to grade-level content will be specific instead of general.

Smarter Balanced Assessment Consortium. The Smarter Balanced Assessment Consortium (Smarter Balanced) calls its achievement category descriptions "achievement level descriptors" (ALDs). Smarter Balanced has four achievement levels. It also has four types of ALDs (Smarter Balanced, 2013a, 2013b). *Policy ALDs* are overall claims about students' progress toward college and career readiness. For example, here is the Policy ALD for Level 4 performance in ELA/Literacy in grade 3:

> The Level 4 student demonstrates thorough understanding of and ability to apply the English language arts and literacy knowledge and skills needed for success in college and careers, as specified in the Common Core State Standards. (Smarter Balanced, 2013a, p. 1)

Content ALDs are written for each content-area claim from the Common Core State Standards—for example, reading closely and analytically to comprehend a range of increasingly complex literary and informational texts. *Range ALDs* are written for item writers and test developers; they define the content range for test items. For example, there are seven targets under reading closely and analytically to comprehend a range of texts. The first target is Key Details, and the Level 4 Range ALD for this target reads as follows:

> Level 4 students should be able to use explicit details and information from the text to support answers or basic inferences in texts of unusually high complexity. (Smarter Balanced, 2013a, p. 1)

Finally, *Threshold ALDs* are written for standard-setting panels. They describe what a student just entering Levels 2, 3, and 4 should be able to do.

Eventually, Smarter Balanced will also have *Reporting ALDs* that describe the knowledge, skills, and processes students demonstrate at each performance level and what knowledge and skills are required to move to the next level. Educators, parents, and students will use these ALDs to interpret students' performance on the Smarter Balanced assessments. However, Smarter Balanced cautions, "These ALDs are not intended to provide guidance to classroom teachers for curriculum or individual student decisions. Such guidance will be provided through the formative assessments" (Smarter Balanced 2013a, p. iii).

Aggregation

Large-scale accountability assessments are made for aggregation, that is, for summarizing results for groups of students. Policy-level decisions require aggregated data—for example, average results for schools and districts. Using scale scores, you can legitimately calculate measures of central tendency and variability—for instance, means, standard deviations, and ranges—because scale scores are interval-level scales. That means each point on the scale is approximately the same "size"—representative of the same amount of achievement—as every other point. The mean and standard deviations are appropriate measures of average performance and variability of performance, respectively, for aggregated data.

Percentages of students at different achievement levels. For tests that also report on achievement categories, as most state tests do, aggregating test scores for a group often means reporting what percent of the group scored at each performance level. This is an intuitive measure and seems like it would be easy to understand. At the surface level, this is true. If 83 percent of students in a given grade this year were Proficient or above in mathematics, and 73 percent were Proficient or above last year, then we can say that more students were Proficient this year than last year.

However, remember that those categories were constructed by using cut scores in a distribution of student performance. The students did *not* perform in lumps or clusters; they performed all along a continuum of achievement described by those scale scores. More students perform near the middle of the distribution than at the extremes. Therefore, cut scores near the middle of the distribution will result in larger, more dramatic changes over time than cut scores near the top or bottom of a distribution (Ho, 2008)—there are simply more students there to shift. Figure 2.2 shows how this works.

The figure shows the simplest case, with one cut score and two achievement categories: Proficient and Not Proficient. Both graphs show a normal curve. The horizontal axis is the score scale, from low on the left to high on the right. The height of the curve represents how many students score at any given location on the scale. The distribution of student achievement on large-scale accountability tests is not necessarily normal, but like a normal curve, such a test will have the bulk of students performing in the middle and fewer students scoring very low or very high.

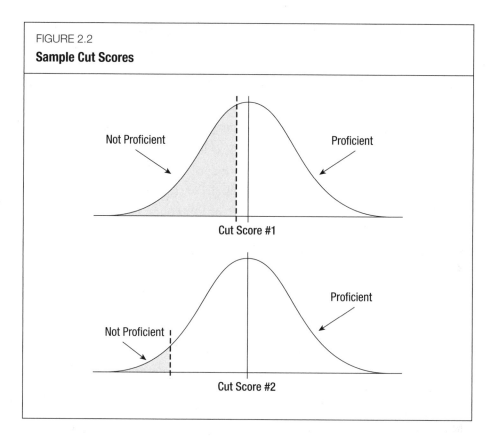

FIGURE 2.2
Sample Cut Scores

Not Proficient

Proficient

Cut Score #1

Proficient

Not Proficient

Cut Score #2

Cut score #1 is set closer to the middle of the distribution than to the extremes. Any student scoring below the cut score, in the shaded area, will be designated Not Proficient. Any student scoring above the cut score will be designated Proficient. You can see that many students score near the cut score because the curve is fairly high there. There will be lots of activity near that cut score—that is, many students will move up a bit in the distribution or down a bit from one year to the next. Any students who cross the cut score— students whose scores may change just a little bit, but right in the neighbor-hood of the cut score so they find themselves on the other side—will cause a change in the percentages of Proficient and Not Proficient students. From one year to the next, then, you would expect dramatic changes in the percent deemed Proficient and Not Proficient, some by chance and some because of small changes in achievement. This shift will happen whether there have been dramatic changes in instruction and learning or not. For example, suppose all students in a school improved by one point. Although this is an improvement, it's not very dramatic. But because there are a lot of students around the cut point, the percentage of Proficient students will rise dramatically. This volatility is a statistical artifact of drawing performance "boxes" (achievement-level categories) around performance that is actually described with a curve.

Cut score #2 is set closer to the extreme low end of the distribution than to the middle. The curve is fairly low at the cut score, meaning there are many fewer students who score in the neighborhood of cut score #2 than cut score #1. Therefore, fewer students will be crossing the cut score next year, even if some major changes in instruction and learning happen.

This same logic applies when there is more than one cut score and there are three or four or five achievement-level categories. The achievement categories with cut scores closer to the middle of the distribution will be more volatile than the ones with cut scores closer to the extremes of the distribution. Interpreting changes in percentages in different achievement categories—something that large-scale accountability tests and public laws and policies tempt educators to do and sometimes even require—is difficult. You usually don't know exactly where in the distribution the cut score falls. Even if you can find that information in a technical report, you still can't tell how much of the change in percentages in your school from last year to this year describes actual improvements in teaching and learning and how much is due to the statistical artifact that I just described.

A cautionary note. The lesson here is clear: Beware interpreting changes in percentages. Gap analyses and trend analyses can be vastly different, even for schools whose students have exactly the same test score distribution, depending on where the cut scores are set (Ho, 2008). In short, analyses based on percentages of students in various achievement categories can be very misleading. So why is that metric part of many reporting laws? I honestly don't know.

Percentages of students at different achievement levels are *status measures*—that is, they describe student achievement at a point in time. Recently, there has been an interest in *growth models*, which describe the nature of changes in achievement from one time point to another.

Growth models

In some ways, it makes a lot of sense to look at growth rather than status in order to evaluate achievement goals for students, schools, and districts. After all, learning is about growing. As we have seen, though, charting growth is not as simple as looking at changes in the percentage of proficient students in different grades or subject areas. That practice is dangerous and can lead to mistaken conclusions. The purpose of this section is to give school- and district-based educators some guidance about how, and how not, to think about growth based on the kind of large-scale accountability data they get from year to year.

Thus in this section I talk about reasonable ways to compare large-scale accountability results from year to year, *not* how to do growth modeling (using "model" to mean a set of rules or calculations for summarizing student performance over time). Most of the time, teachers and administrators do not have a choice about the official growth model used in their state—if there is one, anyway. But they do see large-scale accountability results from year to year.

First, make sure that you don't try to interpret differences in percentages in achievement categories to mean "how much improvement" in terms of the achievement or ability that is assessed (e.g., "how much better in reading"), as we learned in the last section. Rather, comparing percentages answers the question "Did the percentage of students scoring in an achievement category improve?" Comparing percentages gives you only general suggestions about other questions to ask. For example, if your percentages of Proficient and Advanced students are rising in mathematics and declining in reading, you might want to focus on reading and gather more information about reading from data sources in the other three quadrants. But you do not have interpretable information about "how much improvement" has occurred.

Second, focus on the comparison you want to make. Most state assessments do not have a vertical scale, but rather scale performance in each grade separately. That means you can't compare scale scores from grade to grade. Many states do furnish results in the form of percentages in the various achievement levels, and those you can compare, provided that you remember you are comparing *percentages of students* and not *amount of learning*. This is another reason why it's so important to use large-scale accountability results to ask questions, not to make decisions. Let's look at three different ways to compare assessment results, each with different meanings.

Comparing performance in the same year, across grades. This method, shown in the shaded area in Figure 2.3, describes the status of achievement across grades in a school. Whether you are comparing percentages of students in achievement levels or average scale scores, there are different students in each group, and each group took a different test. This kind of comparison doesn't really describe "growth," but rather the status of a particular school at each grade.

Comparing performance in the same grade, across years. This method, shown in the shaded area in Figure 2.4, describes change in performance in a particular grade over time. If you are looking at percentages, the results indicate how percentages of *students* changed, not the amount of change in the subject matter tested. If you are looking at average (mean) vertical scaled scores, as are available for survey achievement batteries such as the Iowa Tests of Basic Skills, you can use the amount of the difference to describe how much change has occurred in the subject matter. However, most state accountability tests don't use vertical scales. And whatever test you are studying, in this comparison there are still different students in each group.

FIGURE 2.3

Comparing Performance in the Same Year, Across Grades

Year	Grade 3	Grade 4	Grade 5	Grade 6
2011				
2012				
2013				
2014				

FIGURE 2.4

Comparing Performance in the Same Grade, Across Years

Year	Grade 3	Grade 4	Grade 5	Grade 6
2011	▓			
2012	▓			
2013	▓			
2014	▓			

Comparing performance of the same group of students across grades. This method is diagrammed in Figure 2.5. Actually, unless no students moved out of or into the class as the years went by, even this design doesn't compare exactly the same groups. In this case you have (almost) the same students, but they still took a different test each year. Standards and curriculum within a domain (e.g., math or reading) change each year. Comparing percentages with this design will allow you to describe how the distribution of students in the various achievement levels changed as the students went through school, but still not how much they learned.

After looking at these three types of comparisons, you may be thinking, "None of these gives me the kind of comparison I need to improve instruction for the students in my school." If you are thinking that, you have made a very wise inference. The primary purpose of large-scale accountability tests is to monitor the performance of *schools*, not students. The goal is to have schools in which a large portion of students in each grade meet

FIGURE 2.5

Comparing Performance of Same Group of Students Across Grades

Year	Grade 3	Grade 4	Grade 5	Grade 6
2011	▓			
2012		▓		
2013			▓	
2014				▓

state standards. When the purpose shifts from policy and administration to instruction—when instead of "how is the school doing?" you want to know "what should we be doing with students?"—you need additional information. Some of that additional information may come from interim/benchmark assessments, but most of it will come from formative and summative *classroom-level* assessments.

More complex ways to describe student growth. All this talk about changes in student performance may have you wondering what kind of growth models are used at the state level for school and teacher accountability. These models are not the topic of this book, but at this point in the discussion it's worth describing what these growth models are and how they differ from the simple comparisons school-level teams make when they look at large-scale data.

The term *growth model* refers to any one of several methods involving calculations, decision rules, or both, that describe change in student learning over time. Growth models require that you have assessments of the same students from at least two points in time. Some growth models describe student learning on an absolute scale, some describe student learning as greater or less than expected, and some predict the amount of expected student learning at some point in the future. When growth models attempt to identify teacher, school, or student characteristics associated with different levels of growth, they are called "value-added" models. Sometimes these teacher, school, or student characteristics are then interpreted as "causing" the growth, which is very hard to justify from statistical modeling alone.

All these growth models require calculations that are not usually feasible for local school districts to do. My purpose in mentioning growth models here is to contrast them with the different kinds of comparisons I just described, which *are* feasible for local schools—as long as you remember the limits and cautions. A comprehensive treatment of growth models is beyond the scope of this book. For a very readable and complete description of different kinds of growth models, I recommend *A Practitioner's Guide to Growth Models* (Castellano & Ho, 2013).

Use of information

The main use of information from large-scale accountability tests is, as I have just shown, for policy and administrative decisions. For example, schools may be identified according to their overall student performance and level of need for targeted assistance.

If you are reading this book, however, you are probably more interested in using large-scale assessment information to improve teaching and learning. The best way to use large-scale information for that purpose is to raise questions suggested by the results. Then do some detective work to find out the answers, using student achievement data from the other three quadrants and information from teachers and students about the nature of instruction, assessment, and learning from multiple points of view.

What You Can (and Can't) Learn from Large-Scale Accountability Assessments

What you can learn from large-scale accountability assessment results depends in part on what kind of results you are interpreting. One of the main points of this section—and one that likely is new to many readers—is that changes in percentages of students in different achievement levels are *not* simple or linear. Percentages of students in achievement categories only give information about the status of students—not the amount of learning—at one point in time. If you don't remember anything else from this chapter, remember that! However, all is not lost. In some of the following examples, I show how generating questions from large-scale accountability results can lead to information that will help improve teaching and learning.

To illustrate how data about student achievement from each of the four quadrants can work together, I'll present two running examples. In this chapter, we'll look at some large-scale accountability information, and then we'll add to the same examples in the chapters about each of the other three quadrants (Chapters 3 through 5). Note that although all of the examples are based on real school data and scenarios, the running examples as a whole are amalgams, and the assessment results do not represent any one specific school.

For the large-scale assessment data, the focus is on questions. First we'll ask, What do we want to know about these results? Then we'll organize the data into a graph or a chart to make it easy to see our preliminary answer. But that answer will go only so far. It will tell us only about performance results. It will not give us the reasons for those results or suggest strategies for improvement.

Therefore, the second focus is on generating questions about possible reasons for the patterns of results that we see in our large-scale accountability data. These, in turn, will lead us to suggest strategies for improvement—but that's getting ahead of ourselves. Those plans require finer-grained information than we have in the results from large-scale accountability assessments.

Example—School 1: Comparing results by subject and disaggregating by groups

In this example, I present state test results for one middle school. Imagine that you are one of the teachers or administrators at this school, and inspect the data table in Figure 2.6. Actually, this table is already considerably streamlined from the spreadsheet of results on the state website. To make it a good starting point for readers of this book, I have already done considerable winnowing.

As you are reflecting on the numbers in the table, remember that the state provides percentages in achievement categories, and you cannot use them to describe how much students know. In fact, it would be better if you didn't have to deal with the percentages at all. We look at them here because, in fact, schools do have to deal with these percentages. Part of the point of this example is knowing how to think about percentages of students in achievement categories without extending that thinking inappropriately.

Probably the first thing you notice is that this is a lot of numbers. And this is only the chart of results for the whole school! We could make three more charts, one for each grade in the building: grade 6, grade 7, and grade 8. For this example, though, we'll use the whole-school results.

These results are reported as percentages of students in four proficiency categories: Advanced, Proficient, Basic, and Below Basic. Remember what we can and can't say when percentages are involved. We can say that,

FIGURE 2.6

Example for School 1: Overall State Test Results for One Year

Student Groups, Math	Number Scored	% Advanced	% Proficient	% Basic	% Below Basic
All Students	749	61.7	23.6	9.9	4.8
Male	396	60.6	25.0	8.3	6.1
Female	353	62.9	22.1	11.6	3.4
White	668	62.7	23.7	9.3	4.3
Black	24	41.7	20.8	20.8	16.7
Hispanic	11	36.4	45.5	18.2	0.0
Asian	32	68.8	15.6	12.5	3.1
Multiethnic	14	50.0	28.6	7.1	14.3
IEP	73	26.0	26.0	21.9	26.0
ELL	7				
Economically Disadvantaged	166	45.8	24.1	21.1	9.0
Student Groups, Reading	Number Scored	% Advanced	% Proficient	% Basic	% Below Basic
All Students	749	49.1	32.2	12.0	6.7
Male	396	44.7	32.1	13.9	9.3
Female	353	54.1	32.3	9.9	3.7
White	668	50.7	31.4	11.8	6.0
Black	24	29.2	37.5	16.7	16.7
Hispanic	11	36.4	45.5	9.1	9.1
Asian	32	43.8	31.3	12.5	12.5
Multiethnic	14	28.6	50.0	14.3	7.1
IEP	73	21.9	21.9	32.9	23.3
ELL	7				
Economically Disadvantaged	166	34.9	34.9	18.7	11.4

Because of rounding error, percentages may not equal 100.

for example, the percentage of students who scored at the Advanced level in math (61.7 percent) is greater than the percentage of students who scored at the Advanced level in reading (49.1 percent). We can't say anything about why. And we can't interpret any changes in percentages next year (for example, if the Advanced reading percentage were to rise) as solely the result of changes in instruction and learning, because the location of the cut score affects changes, too.

Let's notice another thing about percentages. Compare, for example, the percentage of Hispanic students who are Below Basic in math—none!—with the percentage who are Below Basic in reading—9.1 percent, or almost a tenth of all the Hispanic students in the school. But wait a minute. There were only 11 of them. Each student, then, counts as one-eleventh of the group, which is—you guessed it—9.1 percent. The percentage metric becomes almost meaningless when group size is small. The distribution of performance for Hispanic students at this school is almost exactly the same for math and reading. A little over a third, that is, four of them, are Advanced; almost half, or five of them, are Proficient, and two of them are Not Proficient. In math, two students are at the Basic level, and in Reading, one student is at the Basic level and one is Below Basic. (Of course, we are talking about the 11 students as a group. It isn't necessarily true that each individual scored at the same level in math and reading.) Anyway, be careful of making too much of percentages when the number of students is small. In fact, percentages were not even calculated for ELL students in this example because there were only seven of them.

Having made those general points, let's go back to interpreting the whole chart. We need to ask questions and then organize the data to highlight the comparisons in the chart that will answer our questions. For example, we could ask, How do male and female students compare with one another? Or we could ask, How do the distributions for math and reading compare with one another? Or we could ask, How do different ethnic groups compare with one another in mathematics? There are a lot of questions we could ask. Given limited time and energy, which question or questions do we want to focus on?

First, it seems like it might be worth asking, What is the difference in overall group performance between math and reading? That's hard to see in the chart, so we create a data display like the one in Figure 2.7 to highlight this particular question. In any school, there is someone who can do this, even if it isn't you.

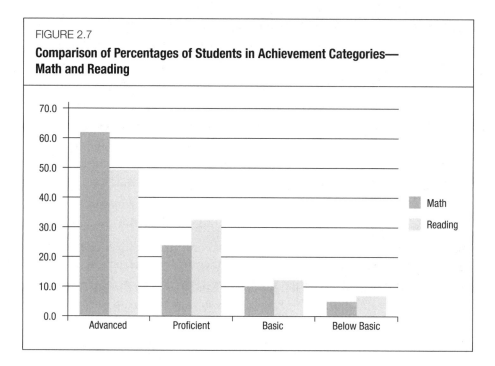

FIGURE 2.7

Comparison of Percentages of Students in Achievement Categories—Math and Reading

This chart highlights the comparison between students' performance in the two subjects. We cannot really conclude students did "better" in mathematics than in reading, in the sense of achievement of certain levels of difficulty of subject matter, but we can conclude that more students are scoring high in mathematics than in reading, and this leads us to the second questioning exercise. Why are students scoring at this level in mathematics? What particular mathematics do they understand? How well is our mathematics curriculum matched to the standards the test measures? We can also ask those questions for reading. We'll have to wait for information from some of the other quadrants to answer these questions. For now, what we have is one question addressed to the data and answered with the chart—How does performance in math and reading compare?—and a set of questions raised by the chart that requires follow-up investigation to answer.

Before we leave this example, let's look at one more chart to further illustrate what we mean by addressing a question to the data and answering it by organizing the information to highlight appropriate comparisons. Suppose that instead of being interested in the difference in subject-area performance, our question had been this: How do economically disadvantaged students compare with our total school population in math performance? Our organization of the data into a chart to highlight the appropriate comparison would have been different, as shown in Figure 2.8. And our follow-up questions would have been different, as well. We might want to know the answers to questions such as these: What mathematics courses are economically disadvantaged students taking? How does that compare with the courses all students are taking? What resources are available to help economically disadvantaged students in mathematics? Do the students take advantage of these? And so on.

The point of showing you two different comparisons from one data chart—and there are many other possibilities—is to demonstrate that the original question you address to the data will shape your follow-up questions, your

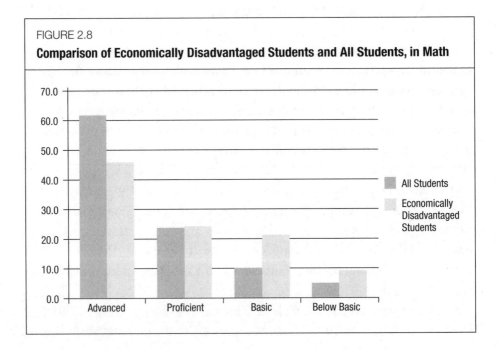

FIGURE 2.8

Comparison of Economically Disadvantaged Students and All Students, in Math

answers, and your ultimate plans for what and how to improve. Therefore, selecting the question you address to the large-scale accountability data is a critical step. No one school can possibly run down all the follow-up questions from all possible looks at the data. Deciding on what comparisons to make is usually a team decision, arrived at after discussion. A school's administration and faculty or data team should be able to explain why they chose to investigate certain results, and not others, from the large-scale accountability test.

Example—School 2: Comparing performance over time

In this example, we present state test score results for a middle school from a different state. This state's data set gives the percentage of students in each of four achievement categories, the percentage of students who scored Proficient or above, as well as the mean and standard deviation of the scale scores for each grade level and subject. The state does not do vertical scaling, so the scale scores are not comparable from grade to grade (e.g., 6th to 7th). However, the scale scores *can* be used to compare average performance within a grade (e.g., 3rd graders this year, 3rd graders next year) for the same test. Scale scores *cannot* be used to compare two subjects (e.g., math and reading).

To keep this example simple, we will only look at the percentage of students who were Proficient or above and the mean scale scores for each year, and only in mathematics (see Figure 2.9). As in the last example, we need to decide what it is we want to know about these results. Let's decide on addressing this question: What has been the pattern of math performance over the

FIGURE 2.9

Four-Year State Test Results:
Percent of Students Proficient or Above in Math, by Grade Level

Grade	Proficient or Above 2010	Mean Scale Score 2010	Proficient or Above 2011	Mean Scale Score 2011	Proficient or Above 2012	Mean Scale Score 2012	Proficient or Above 2013	Mean Scale Score 2013
6	28.8%	618.25	33.9%	621.15	35.7%	623.46	42.7%	626.11
7	23.2%	716.27	25.8%	719.66	26.9%	718.14	47.3%	728.40
8	16.6%	811.35	16.4%	810.76	21.5%	814.71	23.1%	812.19

last four years within each grade? We really wish we had a vertical scale, so we could ask this question about changes from grade to grade. Our question then could have been this: How much change in math knowledge has there been over the last four years? However, we'll use what we have. Figure 2.10 shows a line graph describing mean performance within a grade level across years.

The line graph helps us state the answers to our question. The pattern of math performance has been a slight rise over the last four years for 6th grade. Seventh grade has experienced stable performance over three years, followed by a rise in the last year. Eighth grade performance has remained stable over the four years. This is the information we'll use to write the follow-up questions that we'll use to decide whether there should be changes in instruction.

Before we write those follow-up questions, though, it's worth showing you how interpreting percentages of students in categories is misleading. We can do that because we have both percent-Proficient and mean scale scores for this school. Figure 2.11 shows what the graph would have looked like if we had graphed percent-Proficient instead of mean scale score.

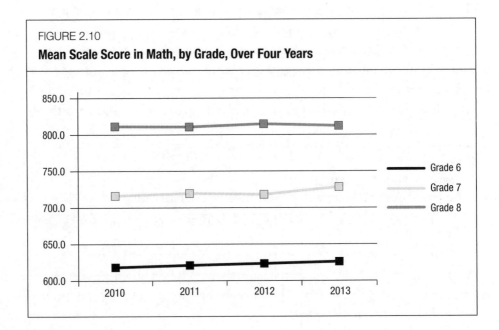

FIGURE 2.10

Mean Scale Score in Math, by Grade, Over Four Years

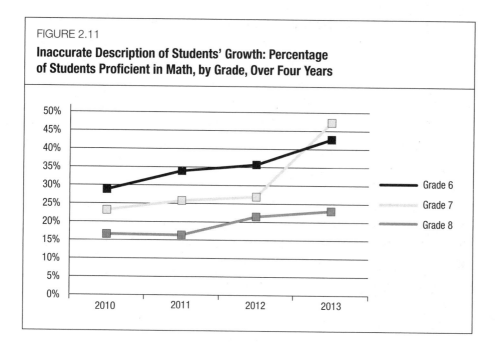

FIGURE 2.11

Inaccurate Description of Students' Growth: Percentage of Students Proficient in Math, by Grade, Over Four Years

If you tried to interpret these changes in percent-Proficient, it would have looked as though mathematics understanding increased substantially in all grades, and that a very dramatic change in instruction had occurred in 7th grade in the last year. Based on the more accurate measure of actual achievement—the scale scores—shown in the first line graph (Figure 2.10), we see that this would have been a mistaken conclusion. There has been recent improvement in 7th grade, and it needs to be followed up, but we would not be looking at a miracle, just a description of modest changes in instruction.

How many schools fall into this trap of misinterpreting percentage changes every year? Lots! Although part of the reason may be not understanding different kinds of data (which is why you're reading this book), I suspect that another part of the reason is that those percentages carry important consequences for schools, so people pay more attention to them than their meaning warrants. The more you know about how to interpret data, the better founded your decisions will be.

Now for the next step. By interpreting the first line graph, we have answered our question to the data: What has been the pattern of math performance over the last four years within each grade? Now comes the step in which we use those answers to generate more questions. Before you read on, stop a minute to think of what questions you might ask.

What happened in 7th grade math classes in 2013? These are not the same students as in 2012, so the change could be partly due to a different group of students. But only 35.7 percent of these students were Proficient in 6th grade, so there might be something else going on, as well. Should we be concerned that 8th grade math achievement is stable? In general, why is mathematics proficiency lower than we might want? What is taught in math classes? How well does the taught curriculum match the state standards as embodied in the test? What do classroom-level assessments, both formative and summative, say about what students know and can do in mathematics? Are students achieving in class but not on the state test, or are they not performing well in class, either?

Concluding Thoughts

Large-scale accountability tests can be the "800-pound gorilla" that spurs schools and districts to all sorts of activity. When that activity is based on an accurate and reasonable appraisal of data, it can be useful. But all too often, schools reason from state test results to some instructional action without doing the follow-up required to ground that action in evidence. Large-scale accountability results are just that—large; and they don't contain any information about the details of learning or instruction that are needed to craft a plan that will actually work.

When I turned 40 years old, a colleague called and left me a voicemail. She yelled into the answering machine: "NOW . . . THAT . . . YOU'RE . . . 40 . . . I'LL . . . MAKE . . . SURE . . . TO . . . TALK . . . TO . . . YOU . . . REALLY . . . LOUD . . . AND . . . SLOW." Funny, right? I laughed when I got the message, and I called her right back to thank her for making me chuckle. But it's not funny when people do essentially the same thing with large-scale accountability results. Those results are loud. And they are cumbersome, because they report on a very large domain—all of the state reporting standards (or priority standards, in some states) in mathematics or reading or science or writing for a grade level.

If you reason directly from large-scale assessment results, about the best you can come up with is the equivalent of "talk louder and slower," something like "work harder in reading" or "spend more time on mathematics." Such responses are not programs for change; they are recipes for disaster. As we all know, repeating or heaping up instruction that isn't working—doing more of the same—is not likely to lead to a different result. For a detailed instructional plan, you need more detailed assessment information. For more detailed assessment information, you need to look at classroom assessment. We'll get there, but first we'll discuss large-scale assessment information that is collected for formative purposes.

3 | Interim/Benchmark Assessments and Common Formative Assessments

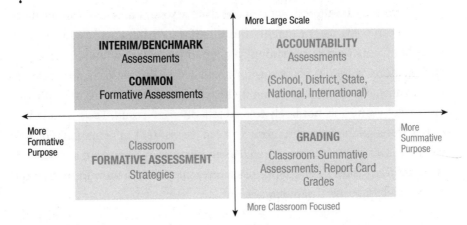

I consider interim or benchmark assessments and common formative assessments to be in the "large-scale/formative" quadrant because they are administered across more than one classroom. Common formative assessments are not usually large-scale in the sense that they have been developed by testing companies and normed, but they are intended for use across classrooms. And to the extent that either interim/benchmark assessments or common formative assessments are used to monitor progress and inform changes in instruction, they are formative.

The terms *interim assessments* and *benchmark assessments* are more or less synonyms. *Interim assessment* emphasizes the predictive function—these assessments are checkpoints on the way to a large-scale accountability test at the end of the school year. The term *benchmark assessment* emphasizes instructional adjustment—these assessments are checkpoints to see whether students are on track in a sequence of intended learning outcomes. Both amount to the same thing. Interim and benchmark assessments are often purchased products and are often administered in six- to nine-week cycles: two, three, or four times a year.

Assessments that are administered as checkpoints during the year are usually intended to do one of three things: inform instruction, predict results of future (e.g., state) assessments, or evaluate curriculum (Perie, Marion, & Gong, 2009). Two of these purposes, informing instruction and predicting future achievement, are clearly formative in nature. Predicting future achievement is "formative" because if the predictions are not satisfactory, then changes in instruction will be made. In fact, most of the uses for interim assessment data do have to do with modifying or adjusting instruction (Abrams & McMillan, 2013; Datnow & Hubbard, 2015).

Currently, little research documents the prediction of state test scores or positive effects on student achievement (Brown & Coughlin, 2007). Because clearly this book emphasizes that classroom formative assessment is much more useful—and should have much more time and energy devoted to it—than interim/benchmark assessment, I looked hard to find a research base for interim assessment so as not to be accused of setting up a straw man. The literature behind the use of classroom formative assessment is so rich, it would be easy to get on the bandwagon with classroom formative assessment and not really give interim assessment a fair hearing. However, I really didn't find much research of substance to support the use of interim/benchmark assessment.

Some published evidence supports the usefulness of interim/benchmark assessment data if used by data teams in schools (Gallimore, Ermeling, Saunders, & Goldenberg, 2009; Saunders, Goldenberg, & Gallimore, 2009). To date, very little research evidence indicates that using interim/benchmark assessments helps improve student achievement. A study from the state of Indiana showed no effects of using interim/benchmark data on student achievement in grades K to 2 and very small effects in grades 3 to 8 (Konstantopoulos, Miller, van der Ploeg, Li, & Traynor, 2011). Most so-called research reports on interim/benchmark assessments describe how data are used or should be used; that is, they are how-to reports rather than studies of effectiveness (Baum, 2011; Goertz, Oláh, & Riggan, 2009; Hamilton et al., 2009; Miami-Dade, 2008). A recent review of research on teachers' use of assessment data to inform instruction found great variability in how teachers analyze and use data and also a tendency for instruction changes to target struggling students, which raises equity issues (Datnow & Hubbard, 2015).

In contrast to interim/benchmark tests, which are standardized tests, *common formative assessments* are usually teacher-made tests that are intended to assess achievement in some particular subject matter across classes in a particular grade. They may be constructed with original items and tasks written by teachers or with items and tasks selected by teachers from item banks. Common formative assessments are likely to be administered with reference to local instruction. For example, a common formative assessment on adding and subtracting fractions might be administered in a school after all the 5th grade teachers have finished teaching that content but while there is still time for additional work, if needed. Here, too, the purpose is formative because the information is intended to change instruction, expanding on strengths and remediating weaknesses.

I want to emphasize the difference between this kind of "formative" purpose and true classroom formative assessment, which is the subject of Chapter 5. Interim and benchmark data, and data from common formative assessment, are intended to form or shape teachers' future instructional plans. These data are for the adults in the educational process. They can be shared with students, and sometimes are, in the form of charts on a wall, for example. But the decisions about what the results mean and what to do about them are made by teachers and administrators. In contrast, students are involved in classroom formative assessment. Students help generate and use classroom formative assessment information. This distinction makes a great deal of difference in the effects of assessment on both learning processes and student motivation.

Some schools use a type of common formative assessment based on student learning outcomes, and thus sometimes called SLOs, as part of a teacher evaluation system (e.g., Illinois State Board of Education, 2013; New York State Education Department, 2014). The term *SLO* can refer to the process that teachers use to select learning objectives by which they will be evaluated, but in common parlance the term has also begun to be associated with the assessments themselves. Not all SLOs are common formative assessments, but in the cases in which teachers select objectives and identify or write assessments to measure them, the assessments amount to something very similar to common formative assessments. Note that our four-quadrant system refers to the functions of various assessments of *student* learning. SLOs, however, are often formative for the student but summative for the teacher, because they are used in teacher evaluation decisions.

Types of Data Available

Interim/benchmark assessments are usually standardized measures, and common formative assessments are often not standardized. Both, however, should assess actionable parts or aspects of state standards, in keeping with their purpose of informing the adjustment of instruction to improve student achievement in specific ways.

Commercial interim or benchmark assessment products can be online assessments, paper-and-pencil tests, or a combination of the two. Some commercial interim/benchmark assessments include item banks. Among the many options available, here are some examples:

- *ACT Aspire* (ACT)—Grades 3–10
- *Acuity* (CTB/McGraw-Hill)—Grades 3–8
- *Pearson Formative Item Bank* (Pearson)—Grades K–12
- *Data Director* (Riverside Publishing)—Grades K–12
- *Edusoft* (Houghton Mifflin Harcourt)—Grades K–12
- *Fountas & Pinnell Benchmark Assessment System* (Houghton Mifflin Harcourt)—Grades Pre-K–2 (system 1) and 3–8 (system 2), Literacy
- *Galileo* (Assessment Technology Incorporated)—Grades K–12
- *Measures of Academic Progress* (*MAP*, Northwest Evaluation Association)—Grades 2–12
- *STAR Assessments* (Renaissance Learning)—Grades K–12
- *TerraNova Math and Reading Assessments* (CTB/McGraw-Hill)—Grades K–12

Some commercial benchmark assessment products are marketed as dual-purpose. They include both benchmark assessments and assessments for more frequent use. The latter can be used for progress monitoring in Response to Intervention (RTI) programs. Examples include the following:

- *aimsweb* (Pearson)—Grades K–8
- *easyCBM* (Riverside)—Grades K–8

Some states have interim assessments as part of their state assessment system. For example, California uses the Smarter Balanced interim assessments (http://www.cde.ca.gov/ta/tg/sa/sbacinterimassess.asp); Michigan has a new interim assessment program as of 2014 (https://www.michigan.gov/mde/0,4615,7-140-22709_63192---,00.html); and Rhode Island has an interim assessment program developed with Race to the Top funds (http://www.ride.ri.gov/InstructionAssessment/Assessment/InterimAssessment.aspx).

The Common Core assessment consortia also include interim/benchmark-type assessments in their assessment systems. The Smarter Balanced Assessment Consortium made interim assessments available to schools in fall 2014, to be administered in intervals of time determined by the local schools or districts (www.smarterbalanced.org/interim-assessments/). There are two options: the Interim Comprehensive Assessment (ICA) and Interim Assessment Blocks (IAB; www.smarterbalanced.org). The ICA is like the Smarter Balanced summative assessment in design, administration, and score reporting. The IAB assesses a smaller set of skills to provide information that is more fine-grained.

PARCC has plans for a diagnostic assessment, "designed to be an indicator of student knowledge and skills so that instruction, supports, and professional development can be tailored to meet student needs" (www.parcconline.org) in grades 3–8 and high school, and a midyear assessment to predict students' performance on the end-of-year summative assessment. Some districts are using the PARCC practice tests as interim assessments.

Domain assessed

To be useful for adjusting instruction, interim/benchmark assessments or common formative assessments need to provide information for smaller domains than just subject areas such as reading and mathematics. Information about these larger domains can be useful for predicting final state test scores, as is the intent of Smarter Balanced's ICA, but they don't help much in answering questions about what content should be retaught or approached from a different angle and what content might be telescoped.

The Measures of Academic Progress (MAP) tests (NWEA, 2012) provide an example of measuring domains at different grain sizes. MAP tests can be administered as "survey with goals tests" or—using fewer items—"survey" tests. The "survey" means the overall score for the test—the large domain, for example, Reading. The "goals" are scores for more specific topics within these areas. For example, there are five goals under Reading (Evaluative Reading Comprehension, Interpretive Reading Comprehension, Literal Reading Comprehension, Literary Response and Analysis, and Word Analysis and Vocabulary Development); five goals under Language Usage (Basic Grammar and Usage, Capitalization, Composing and Writing Process, Composition Structure, and Punctuation); seven goals under Mathematics (Algebraic Concepts; Computation; Geometry; Measurement; Number Sense and Numeration; Problem Solving; and Statistics, Probability, and Graphing); three goals under General Science Topics (Earth and Space Sciences, Life Sciences, and Physical Sciences); and two goals under Science Concepts and Processes (Develop Abilities Needed for Scientific Inquiry and Unifying Processes and Concepts of Science).

As you can see from the titles of the "goals" tests, these subject areas are smaller in scope than the overall test and could provide some direction about instruction. They are still not small-grained enough to be "formative" in the sense we discuss in Chapter 5, where we will see that formative classroom assessment returns information to individual students about what to do next. It's also useful to know that for the MAP, as for any other computer-adaptive test, not all students are presented with the same questions. In computer-adaptive tests, the next item or item set is selected for a particular student based on that student's performance. Students who get items wrong are branched to easier items, whereas students who get items right are branched to more difficult items. Therefore, the sample of performance in even the more specific domains is not consistent from student to student. The title of the test is about as specific a description of the domain as you can confidently report.

Methods and results

When common formative assessments are teacher-made tests or performance assessments, their results are usually expressed in the same metrics as classroom summative assessments. For example, common formative assessments that are tests may result in percentage-correct scores, and performance assessments may result in scores on rubrics that appear as categorical data or as percentages, depending on the scoring scheme used. (See Chapter 4 for a discussion of how to interpret these kinds of data.)

Purchased interim/benchmark assessments yield scores that are like large-scale standardized test scores and *not* like scores on classroom assessments. For example, if you saw a score of *50* on a classroom test, it would probably mean the student got 50 percent, or half, of the test items correct. If you saw a *50* on a standardized test, you would not know without some description of the scale whether that was low, medium, or high on the scale used on the test. A scale score of *50* doesn't mean the student has "50" of anything.

In this section, I'll describe some of the kinds of scores that you might see on interim/benchmark assessments, and on other large-scale assessments, including some state accountability tests and achievement survey batteries. Most commercially available tests describe their scores in test manuals or on their websites, and some provide interpretive aids such as sample problems as well.

Norm-referenced scores. Most large-scale tests yield norm-referenced scores. Even many interim/benchmark tests that describe performance in terms of what a student can do, which sounds criterion-referenced, often have norm-referenced methods at their root. "Norm-referenced" means scores are interpreted by comparing a test score with the scores of individuals in some identifiable group, known as the norm group. The norm group should be defined, and your interpretation should be based in part on the students in the norm group. For example, comparing a student's score to a representative sample of students in the United States in his grade level will lead to an interpretation of his achievement. Comparing the same student's score to a representative sample of students in private schools in the Northeast region of the

United States might lead to another interpretation. Norm-referenced scores stand in contrast to criterion-referenced scores, where the comparison is to an absolute standard or an ordered set of performance descriptions.

Scale scores. A scale score is a score derived from a student's raw score on a test using any one of a number of methods. The resulting scale is arbitrary in the sense that it doesn't represent any particular number of test items or points. The intent of scaling is to add meaning to the score by incorporating more information. In some scales, information about the *mean* (average performance of the group of test-takers) and the *standard deviation* (variability of the group of test-takers) of the scores is incorporated into the formula for deriving a scale score from a raw score. In some scales, information about the difficulty of each question is incorporated into the score. Sometimes, in addition to item difficulty, other information can be incorporated into a scale score—for example, whether the item discriminated well among test-takers with different levels of knowledge or whether the student is likely to have guessed. However, adding this kind of information may result in odd-looking numbers (e.g., decimals with many places or scores with negative numbers). Therefore, scores are often mapped onto more reasonable-looking scales (e.g., 200 to 800) to arrive at the final, reported scale score.

Thus scale scores carry a lot more information than raw scores or simple percentages. As mentioned in Chapter 2 and just described in more detail here, scale scores measure student performance in light of other information. However, that extra information comes at a price. The scale is arbitrary and no longer linked to anything concrete, such as test items or student answers. Sometimes test publishers provide aids to interpretation, such as sample problems that students who scored at a particular level are likely to be able to solve. For example, MAP scores are reported on a scale called a RIT scale (short for Rasch Unit Scale) that ranges from approximately 140 to 300. Interpretation aids called RIT Charts are available that give sample problems students can solve according to their survey scores (NWEA, 2012).

Percentile ranks. Percentile ranks are rankings from 1 to 99. They tell what percent of a norm group scored lower than a particular score. For example, if a student's percentile rank is 82, it means that 82 percent of the norm group had lower scores on the test than that student did. It does *not* mean that the student got 82 percent of the answers correct. The *percent* in *percentile* means percentage of the norm group, not a percentage of anything related to the test items.

Interim/benchmark tests often will provide norms, which are usually in the form of percentile ranks for status (performance on one test) and sometimes for growth (change from test to test). For example, MAP tests provide norms for both status and growth.

When you interpret percentile ranks, it's really important to remember that they are just about ranking, and they don't tell you about what a student actually knows. It's also really important to remember that the composition of the norm group is critical to interpretation. If you found out you were in the 99th percentile on a test of reading comprehension, for example, would that be good news to you? Maybe so, if the norm group was composed of teachers; maybe not, if the norm group was composed of 4th graders.

Another fact to remember when you are interpreting percentile ranks is that different tests have different norming samples. So even if two tests claim they have a "nationally representative sample," you may find that the same student has different percentile ranks on each test. That is normal—pun intended—and expected when you have different samples.

Finally, when you are interpreting percentile ranks, it's important to know that they are *not* an interval scale; that is, they do not represent an equal-interval "ruler" where each point represents the same amount of achievement as every other point. Percentile ranks are closer together in the middle and farther apart at the extremes. It takes a lot more improvement in performance, for example, for a student to move from the 5th to the 10th percentile than to move from the 50th to the 55th percentile. This means you can't add and subtract percentiles, because the units are different sizes.

Aggregation

Unlike data from classroom formative assessments, data from interim/benchmark and common formative assessments can be aggregated. You can, for example, meaningfully talk about "average performance" or the "range of performance" for all students in a certain grade level who took a certain test. Often, for curriculum planning or for evaluating materials or a program, that's exactly what you want to do.

For a teacher-made or locally produced common formative assessment that is scored in terms of percent correct, you can average the percent-correct scores. For example, you could say that the mean score on a teacher-made 4th grade assessment of using details and examples in a text to explain what the text says explicitly and to draw inferences from the text (Common Core ELA Standard RI.4.1) was 80 percent. Don't forget to look at the variability of the scores, as well. If in one school the 4th grade average is 80 percent and performance ranges from 70 percent to 90 percent, and in another school the average is 80 percent and performance ranges from 10 percent to 100 percent, you have two very different pictures of performance. Using an average—whether it's the mean or the median—without looking at the variability only gives you part of the picture.

For interim/benchmark assessments that have scale scores and percentile ranks, average the scale scores. If you need the "average percentile rank," *average the scale scores and then look up what percentile rank is associated with that scale score.* I alluded to the reason for this when I described percentile ranks and scale scores. Scale scores are constructed to have roughly the same amount of "space" between them. That is, the amount of achievement gain from a score of 151 to a score of 152 should be approximately the same as the amount of gain from 152 to 153. However, percentile ranks do not have this property. Percentile ranks are closer together in the middle and more spread out toward the top and bottom of the distribution of scores. When you try to "add up" percentile ranks, you are adding apples and oranges. Of course, your calculator will dutifully return an answer when you punch in numbers, whether they're appropriate numbers or not, so it's up to you to know what numbers to use.

One last point about "average percentile rank." When you average students' scale scores and look up the percentile rank, what you have is the average rank for individual students. You do *not* have the percentile rank of the school. Such a thing can be calculated, but it's a lot more complicated than just averaging individuals. Tables of school average norms were a feature of the traditional multilevel survey battery tests (such as the *Iowa Tests of Basic Skills*) but are not much used in interim/benchmark tests, where the focus tends to be on the performance of individual students and the aggregated performance of various groups of students.

Use of information

The use of interim assessments is widespread but recent, so research on how teachers actually use interim assessment information is limited. Teachers mostly use interim assessment data for remediating individuals or small groups of students, reteaching particular content to a whole class, or grouping students (Abrams & McMillan, 2013).

In one study (Riggan & Oláh, 2011), teachers in grades 3 and 5 in Philadelphia and Cumberland, Pennsylvania, used interim assessment data to identify either content or students in need of further work or remediation. When they identified content areas of note in interim assessments, teachers mapped them back to content standards. In either case, whether the focus was on the content or on individual students, teachers sought additional information about why students gave the answers they did by using short-cycle assessment, or what I, in this book, have been calling classroom formative assessment. Thus the interim assessment data did not directly influence a decision, but rather pointed teachers to an area of investigation and prompted looking at additional assessment data.

This description of teachers' use of interim assessment data is exemplary as far as it goes. However, several studies provide evidence that teachers often stop at figuring out what content to reteach or which students to help and are less likely to take the next step and decide on changes in instructional methods (Abrams & McMillan, 2013; Goertz, Oláh, & Riggan, 2009). As my principal used to say to me when I was a classroom teacher, "If something didn't work for a student before, what are you going to do differently this time?" Repeating or reteaching content without changing instructional methods is likely to result in the same learning (or lack of it) that resulted in the first place.

There is also some evidence that teachers use interim assessment for purposes that are not recommended. For example, Blanc and her colleagues (2010) found that teachers used interim assessment data to identify "bubble kids," or students on the verge of moving from one proficiency level to another, to target them for specific instruction. The teachers in this study also reported using interim assessment data to identify content for reteaching and to identify students with similar deficits for grouping.

In each of these studies, there seems to be a focus on deficit thinking, looking for content areas or students who are wanting in some way. That's an occupational hazard that comes when any school takes a triage approach to assessment and accountability. Good assessment data should be so much more, describing a picture of strengths and weaknesses and motivating a closer look at classroom-level data *and* at instructional methods (Boudett, City, & Murnane, 2013).

In summary, we can make two main points about the use of interim assessment information. First, interim assessment is primarily used to raise red flags, identifying either content areas or specific students for further investigation using classroom-level data, primarily classroom formative assessment. This function is a good thing because changes in instruction are best made when you understand *why* students think the way they do about specific content. Second, interim assessment has not, to date, shown any potential to change instruction, and that means that either interim assessment is not living up to its potential or the potential wasn't there in the first place. In the next section, I'll have more to say about that.

What You Can (and Can't) Learn from Interim/Benchmark Assessments and Common Formative Assessments

We'll have to talk about interim/benchmark assessments and common formative assessments separately, because what you can learn from each is a bit different. We'll start with interim/benchmark assessments to continue the discussion we started in the last section.

What you can learn from interim/benchmark assessments

Because interim/benchmark assessments provide information on student achievement at a grain size smaller than whole subject areas but larger than classroom learning objectives, it really is necessary to use the data as a source of questions that lead to looking for more information, rather than as a source of answers about how instruction needs to change. The data as they stand are too coarse for anything but the broadest instructional decisions—for example, to spend more time on a particular content area.

So what you learn from interim/benchmark assessments depends in large part on the quality of your questions. If they remain at the level of "Who needs help to show up as Proficient?" you will not learn much, and you risk using the data in a punitive manner. I remember talking with a middle school principal who was excited about using "flex groups," by which he meant homogeneous—in the sense that they all fell short of proficiency on a particular state standard—groups of students. Hmm. Think about that: Let's take a group of students who aren't good at something and probably therefore don't like it very much, put them all together in a homogeneous group so none of them can help each other, and make them do more of the same work they can't do and don't like. Does this sound like an effective strategy?

But if your questions are thoughtful, you will get further. For example, you may ask, "Why do our students do well on literal reading comprehension but not as well on literary response and analysis?" That question will lead you to a brainstorming session with the teachers who teach literature. How might they explain that result? Analysis of literature is a feature of the Common Core State Standards, and it differs from the kind of reading comprehension many teachers may have spent most of their time on in previous years. Are teachers spending more time on literal comprehension than on analysis (in which case, both instructional time and pacing and instructional methods might need to change)? Or are they spending time on analysis with little student learning to show for it (in which case, instructional methods might be the focus for change)? What do classroom assessments of literary analysis look like? Do they truly require analysis-level thinking, or are they just extended exercises in literal comprehension? What does student work look like on these classroom measures?

As you can tell, these questions require an honest look at classroom instruction and at the work students are asked to do. Getting information of this sort to support instructional improvement and, ultimately, improved student achievement requires a climate that focuses on learning and not evaluation. And this, as suggested earlier, is what I suspect is the reason interim/benchmark assessments have not really resulted in much change in instruction. In an evaluative climate, interim assessments can be used as "quizzes" or "checkups" with an emphasis on finding out what is "wrong." This kind of climate doesn't support honest reflection on classroom instruction—or anything else, for that matter. Rather, it produces defensiveness.

What you can learn from common formative assessments

Common formative assessments *can* give much more targeted information than interim/benchmark assessments, because they are—or at least are supposed to be—directly tied to curriculum as taught in a particular grade in a particular school or district. That's a big *if*, however.

The quality of the information you get from a common formative assessment depends on the quality of the assessment. I have seen common formative assessments that were well constructed and some that were not. One problem I have noticed in some common formative assessments is weighting that is out of whack. Most common formative assessments cover a set of learning objectives, and the portion of the assessment's score devoted to each objective should be proportional to the importance of each. In addition, at least some of the assessment items or tasks should be pitched at cognitive levels appropriate to the learning objectives. For example, if an objective calls for students to be able to analyze the structure an author uses to organize a text, assessment items or tasks should call for analysis-level thinking. Once you're sure each content area/learning objective and cognitive level is appropriately represented in the mix that determines the assessment's score, you also need to be sure that the items or tasks and the rubrics or other scoring schemes appropriately capture that performance—that they are well written and well crafted.

If you have confidence in the quality of your common formative assessment, you should be able to get actionable information from it. Because the learning objectives and the thinking skills represent what you taught, you can compare student performance, individually or by class or other groupings, to your expectations. Areas where performance exceeded expectations or failed to meet expectations become areas for modifying instruction. And because the expectations were based on your own instruction, you should have more ideas about exactly what to modify than you do with interim/benchmark assessment results. However, similar to the information from interim/benchmark assessments, information from common formative assessments is better at identifying areas that need change (e.g., a particular objective that students didn't learn as well as you intended) than at describing student thinking. For that information, you still need to supplement your common formative assessment results by looking at classroom formative assessments.

Let's return to the examples we began in Chapter 2. In both examples, a school organized some large-scale accountability data in order to highlight a particular comparison the educators were interested in. Then the educators used the results of those analyses to raise follow-up questions they thought might help them plan for improvement of instruction and learning in their school.

Example—School 1

The school in the first example concluded that more students were scoring well in mathematics than in reading. The follow-up questions began with analyzing *why.* What particular mathematics do the students understand? How well is the mathematics curriculum matched to the standards the test measures? What particular reading outcomes have they mastered? How well is the reading curriculum matched to the standards the test measures?

Educators in this school could look at MAP data for partial answers to the questions about math and reading achievement. They had used the survey version of MAP, so they had data from fall, winter, and spring on overall reading and mathematics interim assessments. They located a resource on the MAP website that reported on a study predicting student performance on the state test. This resource included MAP cut scores for fall and spring that predicted likely performance at the Advanced, Proficient, Basic, and Below Basic levels on the state accountability test. Reviewing these, they found that the MAP predictions accorded fairly well with the students' performance and that, according to their scores on this benchmark test, more students had been predicted to score at the Advanced level in mathematics than in reading.

This school still needs to pursue its follow-up questions about specific student achievement with classroom assessment information. It also needs to check its curriculum to see if it aligns with state standards and to check with teachers to see whether the taught curriculum reflects the intended curriculum with fidelity.

Example—School 2

Educators in the second school were concerned that students showed lower than desired performance in math. Their follow-up questions included these: What happened in 7th grade math classes in 2012, when performance rose? Should we be concerned that 8th grade math achievement is stable? In general, why is mathematics proficiency lower than we might want? Are students achieving in class but not on the state test, or are they not performing well in class, either?

This school had administered teacher-developed common formative assessments during the year, so it had assessment information linked to the content of the curriculum and the time it was taught. These assessments used percent-correct scoring. In 7th grade, topics assessed had included ratios and proportions; multiplying and dividing fractions; basic geometry, including area and volume; and probability. Students had done well enough in all these areas. Ratios and proportions had been the most difficult of these topics for students, as indicated by the lowest mean percent-correct score on that test, overall and for each math class separately. Still, average performance had hovered around the 85 percent mark for most of the topics and 80 percent for ratios and proportions, suggesting more mathematics learning than reflected in the state accountability test scores.

Taking a closer look at the questions on the common formative assessments, teachers found that all of the questions were at the Apply level.

Problems were mostly routine in nature, and solving them required students to recognize the "kind of problem" as taught in class and then apply a solution strategy taught in class. To solve these problems, students did not need to recognize patterns in numbers, make inferences, or explain their reasoning. Students were not asked to represent concepts in more than one way (e.g., mathematical expressions, graphs, tables, diagrams, words, pictures). Some of the problems on the state test required students to define a problem, to solve a problem in more than one way, and to explain their reasoning. Teachers began to wonder if lack of opportunity to learn and practice mathematical thinking was one of the reasons for the state mathematics results. They added this possibility to their list of follow-up questions to check against classroom-level data.

Concluding Thoughts

Understanding the information available from interim/benchmark and common formative assessments is important for understanding the whole of an assessment system. As you may have concluded from the examples, however, a lot more development in this area will be needed before they provide much more information than is available from state accountability assessments. Some people, myself included, believe that time and energy for assessment development would be better spent improving classroom-level formative and summative assessment. Because classroom assessments are much finer-grained and much closer to the learning than large-scale assessments, and because they can affect student motivation as well as achievement, they are likely to be much more useful for students and teachers (Shepard, 2006). The next two chapters discuss classroom-level assessment: classroom summative assessment, or grading, in Chapter 4, and classroom formative assessment in Chapter 5.

Classroom Grades | 4

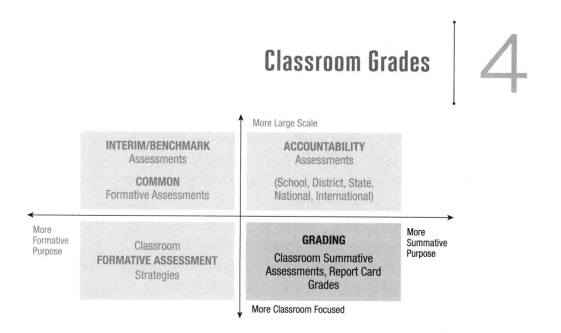

At certain points during learning—at the end of a unit, for example, or at the end of a section of a unit—students take assessments that are graded. These can be tests or performance assessments. A test is a collection of items to which the students respond either by selecting an answer from a set of choices (e.g., multiple choice, true-false, matching) or by constructing an answer (e.g., a focused essay question or a show-the-work problem). A performance assessment consists of a task that engages a student in demonstrating a process (e.g., playing a G-major scale on the clarinet) or creating a product (e.g., writing a report, making a map) and a scoring scheme (e.g., rubrics) that provides for systematic observation and judgment of that performance.

At the end of report periods (often but not always every nine weeks), teachers aggregate graded assignments into report card grades. These are called "composite" grades because they are composed of a set of grades on individual assignments. As you can imagine, the meaning of report card grades depends on the quality of two things: the quality of the original grades on each assessment, and the method teachers use to put the grades together.

Types of Data Available

Grading methods range widely. Historically, classroom grades have been found to be unreliable, although they can be made more reliable with the use of clear criteria and attention to scoring consistently (Brookhart, in press). Because teachers' grading practices vary so widely, it is not possible to develop an exhaustive list of the types of data available from grades, but the following list covers the most common ways teachers produce "data" (grades) from individual assessments of student work:

• Tests that allocate points to each answer, add up points earned, and divide by total possible points, for a percent-correct score.

• Performance assessments that apply rubrics to student work. The total grade is an average performance level across all the criteria (e.g., Proficient).

• Performance assessments that apply rubrics to student work. The total grade is calculated as the sum of points earned on each criterion divided by total possible points. Although this method is not recommended except for rubrics with a very large number of points (Brookhart, 2011), it is used often.

The final format of composite report card grades is a matter of district policy. But how individual assessment results are combined to arrive at the report card grade is usually left up to the teacher. Methods vary widely and, again, it is not possible to list them all. The most common methods for calculating report card grades include the following:

• Put all individual assessment results on the same scale (e.g., percentages, *ABCDF*, proficiency levels) and take the average (mean or median).

• Assign a certain number of total points to each assignment, balancing the importance of each; add up the points students earned; and use either percentages or cutoff scores to assign grades.

The resulting report card grades yield information that differs from large-scale test scores, and from classroom formative assessment, in at least five ways:

1. Report card grades assess learning outcomes at a medium grain size—the reporting standards (or what was intended to be taught and learned) for the report period. Standards-based grades indicate more detailed information (e.g., "tells time") than traditional grades (e.g., "mathematics"), but still summarize learning over one report period.

2. The type of achievement indicated by report card grades is school-based achievement. School-based achievement and achievement as measured by standardized tests are different and are only moderately related (Brookhart, in press).

3. Report card grades are usually different for each class, because the "ingredients" (the individual assignments or assessments) on which they are based differ by class.

4. Report card grades are based on a mixture of teacher-made and teacher-selected (e.g., a test from a textbook series) assessment items or tasks.

5. The primary users of information from report card grades are students and their teachers.

These characteristics of report card grades affect the meaning of the data that the strategies yield.

Domain assessed

Individual graded assessments usually aim to assess content knowledge and skills at the level of unit goals. For example, at the end of a social studies unit on World War II, a test might expect students to know facts about that period in history and to use that knowledge to analyze or explain some events in that period or the period just following.

What report card grades assess depends on the type of report card. For districts using standards-based report cards, the report card grade aims to assess content on reporting standards. In some cases, these may be the same as state standards, but often they are more focused and reflect the portion of the state standards intended to be taught and learned in the particular report period. For example, a 3rd grade report card might specify "adds and subtracts 3-digit numbers" and "knows multiplication and division facts to 10" (Brookhart, 2011). The set of individual grades that is aggregated to make this composite grade would consist of graded assessments for that reporting standard during that report period.

In districts that use more traditional report cards, the report card grade aims to assess, in more general terms, what was studied in a particular subject area (e.g., mathematics, English) during that report period. The set of individual grades that is aggregated to make this composite grade would consist of all graded assessments in that subject during that report period.

Research on classroom grades is one of the oldest fields of study in educational assessment. Studies from more than 100 years have shown that people have always expected grades to measure "achievement." For decades, however, studies have reported correlations between grades and standardized test scores in the .40 to .70 range, which means tested achievement explains no more than half the variance in graded achievement, and sometimes less than that. Even given that some of the difference is due to inexpert grading practices on the part of some teachers, that's too much difference to pronounce that "graded achievement" is supposed to mean the same thing as "tested achievement." In high school, graded achievement gets closer to tested achievement, but graded achievement still reflects a wider array of learning outcomes than standardized tests measure, and it includes information about how students are socialized into the way learning happens in classrooms (Brookhart, in press).

Methods and results

Test scores or percentages and rubrics or other categorical data are very different kinds of numbers. These differences affect how you interpret grades and how you use them in further analysis.

Test scores, percentages, and other point-based grades. The kind of grading that uses a "test-score" approach, in which each item or part of a task is worth a certain number of points and those points are added up for a total, leads to numbers that can be thought of as existing on a continuum. This continuum is <u>not exactly a</u> "ruler," because there is no true zero <u>point</u>. (Getting zero points doesn't mean the student's head is completely empty of any learning in the domain tested, it just means the student didn't know enough to get any question right; whereas the zero mark on a ruler indicates a total absence of length.) This is true for individual assessment results, and it's also true for report card grades that are expressed as percentages, as many high school report cards still are.

Why is this something that's important to know when you are working with data? It's important because of what you can—and can't—defensibly do when you are analyzing this kind of data. You can add and subtract meaningfully with this kind of data. For example, you can say that a student who got a score of 90 percent got "30 percentage points more" than the student who got a score of 60 percent. But you cannot multiply or divide meaningfully with this kind of data. For example, you can't say that the student who got a score of 90 percent has achieved "one and a half times as much" as the student who got a score of 60 percent.

Your calculator won't know the difference: key in 90 divided by 60 and it will return 1.5. You have to know what you can and can't do with the kind of data you have. Many people just assume all numbers work the way they were taught in elementary school when they learned their math facts. But they don't! As the title of this book says, there are different kinds of data. And when you make decisions based on invalid analyses, you can get into trouble. You may think the data mean something that they don't.

Rubrics and other categorical grades. When assessments are scored with rubrics that have relatively short scales (e.g., 1 to 4 or 1 to 6, or something like that), or when assessments are scored directly onto a letter-grade scale (e.g., a student receives a paper that is marked simply with a *B*) or a proficiency scale (e.g., Advanced, Proficient, Basic, Below Basic), the data are called *ordinal*. That means that even if you use numbers rather than words, the grade represents <u>achievement on a scale of ordered categories</u>. There is no guarantee that the "amount of achievement" encompassed in the range of performance that would be called "Advanced," for example, is the same "amount of achievement" encompassed in the range of performance that would be called "Proficient." When report card grades are reported on a categorical scale (*ABCDF* or a proficiency scale), even if they included some tests that were originally graded with points and percentages, they become ordinal or ordered-category data.

If some of the data you are looking at include student grades, it's important to know that you can't add, subtract, multiply, or divide them. For example, if one student scores a 4 and another a 2, it does not follow that the first student achieved competence in twice as much of the domain (e.g., reading). It doesn't even follow that the first student is "2 points better" than the second. What you can legitimately conclude is that the first student is better—has achieved more—in that domain, but you can't say by how much.

Aggregation

Grades can be aggregated if you're careful how you do it. For percentages, you can take the mean. (The mean is what most people think of when you say "average," but really it's only one kind of average.) For example, you can say the average grade on that test in this class was 84 percent, arrived at by adding up the test score for each student in the class and dividing by the number of students.

For letter grades or any other categorical grades, the most defensible aggregation method is to take the median. For example, you can say that the median grade for a writing assessment in your class that was scored with a 6-point rubric was a 4, arrived at by lining up all the scores in order and finding the middle of that set of scores.

All of us who have graduated from high school are familiar with a way of aggregating grades called the "cumulative grade-point average," often abbreviated as GPA. Final course grades are assigned numbers (e.g., *A* = 4, *B* = 3, and so on), weighted according to level and number of credits earned, then averaged by taking the mean. Think about what happens to the meaning of the grades as "data" when you do this. Averaging together grades from English language arts, mathematics, science, social studies, foreign language, and other courses removes grades' ability to reference particular learning outcomes in a course—which is what they started out to measure.

If school (graded) achievement measures a wider array of learning outcomes than standardized tests measure and includes information about how students are socialized into the way learning happens in classrooms, and if the GPA "amalgam" averages across these, what is left is a measure of how well students did in school in general, with an emphasis on how they are socialized in classroom learning (because that part is in all of the grades, whereas the learning outcomes are different for each course). In other words, creating a GPA entails putting measures of achievement of different course outcomes into the same pot and results in a measure of what we might call "studenting."

Studenting is a useful construct for some purposes. If you're looking to predict future educational actions, having a measure of "being a student" is more what you want than a measure of any particular learning. Research bears out that grades are important predictors of dropping out of school (Bowers, 2010; Bowers & Sprott, 2012; Bowers, Sprott, & Taff, 2013) and of taking a college entrance exam (Bowers, 2010). Grades predict college admission, college performance, and college graduation (Atkinson & Geiser, 2009; Thorsen & Cliffordson, 2012) and are especially useful in situations involving low selectivity (Sawyer, 2013). This finding means grades are especially important for the future of average and lower-achieving students. As Pattison, Grodsky, & Muller (2013) summarize, "Grades are the fundamental currency of our educational system; they signal academic achievement and noncognitive skills to parents, employers, postsecondary gatekeepers, and students themselves" (p. 259). Despite changes in grades and concerns about "grade inflation," the signaling power of grades has remained constant over many decades (Pattison, Grodsky, & Muller, 2013).

Use of information

The primary users of grades as information are students, parents, and teachers, primarily for decisions about individual students. Using grades as part of the basis for data-based decision making brings us back to our theme of different kinds of data. This chapter has shown that, in general and assuming sound grading practices, grades on individual assessments measure student achievement of unit goals; course grades measure student achievement of course objectives; and grade-point averages measure general "studenting" or success in school. Be sure to look at the particular kind of grades that answer your question.

For example, if your school has noticed that 3rd grade mathematics results are not what you expected and that problem solving seems to be a particular issue, the most relevant grades to look at are grades on individual assessments of mathematics problem solving. Mathematics course grades would include problem solving but would also include computation and other mathematics skills. So first you have to find out whether there *were* any graded assessments of mathematics problem solving, and if so, what kinds of problems were on the test. Looking at what was graded can be as instructive as looking at the grades themselves (you would do both), assuming that what was assessed reflects what was taught.

What You Can (and Can't) Learn from Classroom and Report Card Grades

Grades from individual classroom assessments support general conclusions made from large-scale test scores and can provide valuable additional information to make those general conclusions more instructionally actionable. For example, if a general conclusion from a state writing test was "students don't write as well as we wish," classroom grades on specific writing assignments can fill in some specifics. What kinds of writing did students do, and with what results (grades)? It might be, for example, that students' narrative writing was better than their expository writing. Or, for another example, if students' large-scale mathematics scores were low on average, scores on mathematics unit tests and other assessments might help pinpoint what particular mathematical content needed more attention.

Report card grades can be used to support general conclusions from large-scale test scores, as well. In addition, with or without large-scale assessment information, report card grades can support program evaluation. The distribution of grades—for instance, a graph of how many *A*s, *B*s, *C*s, *D*s, and *F*s were received in a course—provides a picture of both the level of achievement in a course and how spread out the achievement was. In general, one would expect a negatively skewed distribution, with most of the grades at the passing level, showing that most students met standards and curricular objectives and few failed. Figure 4.1 shows an example of what that looks like.

In fact, in schools that use traditional grading (*ABCDF*, as opposed to standards-based grading), often *B* is the average grade in a class. This can be an issue in itself, because traditional grading scales often label *C* as "average." Parents whose children bring home *C*s can be thinking their students are achieving in the middle of the pack when they are not (Waltman & Frisbie, 1994).

Courses that do not follow this pattern can be examined in more depth to find out why many students did not pass, or why every student received the same grade, for example. Potential reasons could include a change in curriculum, students, or teacher. Let me be clear that the point is *not* that you

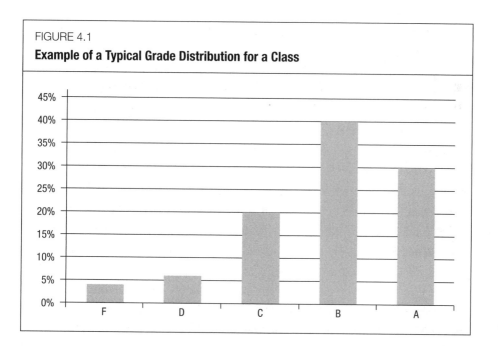

FIGURE 4.1

Example of a Typical Grade Distribution for a Class

want to "engineer" grades to have a desired distribution. Rather, you gather information to help interpret a grade distribution, which is usually the result of an interaction of curriculum, students, and teacher. Interpretations of grade distributions might suggest changes in program (curriculum or materials, or both), students (who enrolls in the course), or teacher (instructional methods).

Let's remind ourselves again of our running examples. School 1 had state test results that suggested higher achievement in mathematics than in reading. School 2 had state test results that suggested lower than desirable achievement in mathematics. What information from students' grades and graded work can help them with their follow-up questions and, ultimately, action plans for improvement?

Example—School 1

Educators in School 1 wondered why their students were scoring at the Advanced level in mathematics at a higher rate than in reading. With just percentages, they couldn't be sure students really had achieved more in math than in reading, but they still wanted to see those percentages rise in reading. An examination of their benchmark test results told them these results had been predictable, and therefore should not have been surprising. Because the same group of students took both tests, differences in students couldn't have caused the difference in performance. To follow up, the school was investigating the following questions: Can we find a reason for the discrepancy in performance? What particular mathematics do students understand? How well is the mathematics curriculum matched to the standards the test measures? What particular reading outcomes have students mastered? How well is the reading curriculum matched to the standards the test measures?

The distribution of the English language arts/reading and mathematics grades for students in this middle school suggested that students were performing better overall in mathematics than in reading, but not dramatically so (see Figure 4.2). Along with the benchmark test results, this highly aggregated view suggested that the pattern in the state test scores was reflective of something that was happening in the school. The difference in state test results between reading and mathematics probably looked more dramatic than the

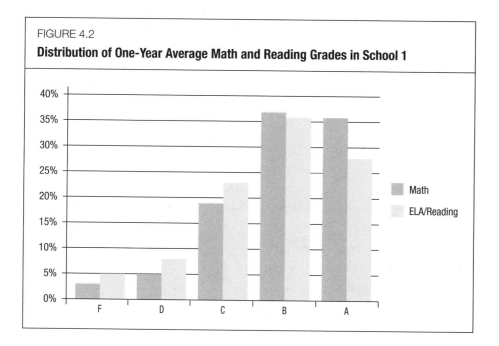

FIGURE 4.2

Distribution of One-Year Average Math and Reading Grades in School 1

differences in students' actual learning because of the volatile nature of the measure, percentages in categories. The question remained, then: What is the nature of this difference?

Looking at individual graded work came next. Grades on individual tests and projects generally reflected the same pattern as the overall distribution of grades, so that examination didn't offer any additional explanation. Looking at what the students were asked to do on the tests and projects, however, was very enlightening.

In English/language arts classes, the bulk of graded work in reading came from "story tests" that required students to answer literal and inferential comprehension questions from stories they had read in their reading books. Few questions asked about authors' purposes. Students were also graded on completing free-reading journals that basically consisted of a list of what they had selected to read and a short synopsis of the story, article, or book. Students' graded work included no comparative analyses of two different texts and very few assignments requiring an analysis of how a text or story was applicable in students' own lives.

In mathematics, test grades formed the bulk of students' graded work. The problems on the tests required students to show and explain their work. In fact, for good or for ill, the math teachers said they used that kind of problem because that kind of thinking was required for the state test. Students were explicitly taught how to explain their work and sometimes were required to do it with different representations (e.g., with words and also with diagrams).

The educators at School 1 made a tentative hypothesis. They speculated that the reason students scored at the Advanced level more in mathematics than in reading on the state test was that students were being asked to do more conceptual thinking—defining a problem and linking it to a solution strategy—and communicating in mathematics. Metacognitive thinking was engaged as students worked to understand and explain their own thought processes. These skills, along with the mathematical computation needed to do the problems, matched what the state standards required and the state test assessed. In contrast, in reading, students' thinking was mostly limited to literal and inferential comprehension of individual passages. There were few opportunities to analyze meaning across texts, evaluate the success of authors' uses of various literary devices, or discuss authors' purposes. Therefore, what students were graded on in reading was only a partial match with what the state standards required and the state test assessed.

Example—School 2

The school in the second example was concerned the students showed lower than desired performance in math, despite some improvement in the 7th grade in 2012. Educators wondered what happened in 7th grade math classes in 2012 and, more generally, why students' test results showed lower mathematics proficiency than they would like, at all grade levels. Were students achieving in class but not on the state test, or were they not performing well in class, either? The educators in School 2 decided a look at students' grades would help answer that last question. They also decided to look at the most recent year, for which people's memories would be fresher. Figure 4.3 shows what they found.

A look at students' overall grades for the year in mathematics at each grade level suggested that students' grades in mathematics were a cause for concern. Students in 7th grade did have a higher percentage of *A*s (24 percent) than students in grades 6 or 8. However, students' grades at all three grade levels painted a rosier picture of student learning than did the state test results. More than half of the students were not Proficient on the state test, but only a little over a quarter of the students' grades were at the *D* or *F* level. Was classroom-graded work simply easier than the state test? Was the work students were graded on only a partial match with the state standards in mathematics? Or was the answer maybe a little of both?

To answer these questions, teachers in School 2 looked at the individual assessments that went into the overall report card grades. As in School 1, they found that tests comprised most of the graded work in mathematics, and that

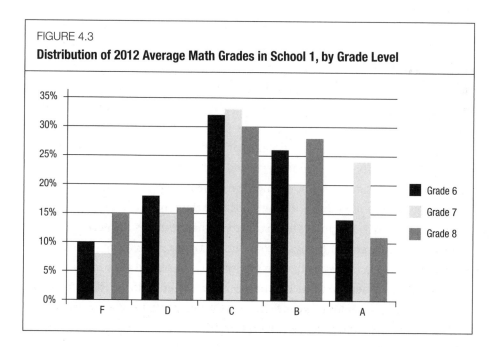

FIGURE 4.3

Distribution of 2012 Average Math Grades in School 1, by Grade Level

students' grade distributions on the tests were very similar to the overall grade distribution they had just graphed.

Looking at the questions on the math tests showed several things. First, most of the tests presented a homogeneous set of problems just like the ones students had studied in class. Nothing in students' grades reflected whether they could figure out for themselves what kind of problem they were dealing with and bring an effective solution strategy to bear. Problem type was a given on each math test. Second, on most tests, problems were graded according to whether the answer was right or wrong and was presented in the correct format (e.g., with labeled answers). Students had no opportunity to explain mathematical reasoning. Thus the teachers in School 2 decided the answer to their question was "a little bit of both." Math tests in school were generally easier than the state test. And they required mostly routine application of solution strategies as taught in class, which was only a partial match with the state standards and the state assessment.

Based on the distribution of grades, however, the students didn't find the mathematics easy: about a quarter of them were doing unsatisfactory work. Classroom formative assessments would give these teachers evidence about what kind of thinking students were doing in mathematics and why they found relatively simple work challenging.

Concluding Thoughts

Using grades as a source of data is a bit tricky, because usually teachers control the contents of classroom tests and performance assessments and how grades are assigned. Most teachers use assessments that they think are appropriate and grade them with methods that they think are appropriate. Therefore, although the analyses described in the examples for School 1 and School 2 are fairly straightforward to describe, they are anything but straightforward to do. I can attest to that. In one school I observed a middle school social studies teacher look at a 10-question test he had written, in which each answer was a date ("In what year did . . .?"), and insist that it was a good test and his students had to think deeply to pass it!

Analyzing grades and classroom assessments takes a lot of collaboration and a high level of professional expertise and judgment. But that shouldn't be bad news. A focus on data to make decisions about improvements in learning can be a vehicle for improving schoolwide collaboration skills and for professional development in assessment. If your school needs improvement in these areas, it might be wise for a colleague who is knowledgeable in assessment to lead data sessions with professional development goals as well as goals for interpreting students' achievement.

In the next chapter we turn to classroom formative assessment. As a source of data, classroom formative assessment can be messy because you are trying to look at student thinking—at what is going on "inside a kid's head"—and not at tables of numbers that can be organized into clear graphs or charts. However, classroom formative assessment is also the richest source of data, precisely because it can give you a window into student thinking and thus valuable evidence about the process of student learning.

5 | Classroom Formative Assessment Strategies

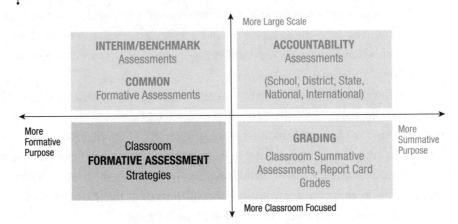

Classroom formative assessment is "an active and intentional learning process that partners the teacher and the students to continuously and systematically gather evidence of learning with the express goal of improving student achievement" (Moss & Brookhart, 2009, p. 6). Others have expressed the definition of formative assessment in similar terms (Andrade, 2010; Black & Wiliam, 2009; Third International Conference on Assessment for Learning, 2009).

Unpacking this definition, we can notice several things. Formative assessment strategies are intended to help illustrate for students what a particular learning target or goal means, develop their capabilities as they work, and provide feedback—from self, teacher, or others—to guide their way forward by illuminating their next steps in learning. Students and teachers are involved in formative assessment. No matter whether the direction comes from teachers or from students (Andrade, 2010; Brookhart, 2001), the purpose of formative assessment is increased student learning. Therefore, the results from formative assessment, the "data," if you will, are the feedback or student insights that inform future learning.

When done well, the formative assessment process increases both student learning and motivation (Black & Wiliam, 1998; Brookhart, 2007; Kingston & Nash, 2011). For example, Ross, Hogaboam-Gray, and Rolheiser (2002) investigated the effects of clear criteria and self-evaluation on mathematics problem solving. A self-evaluation treatment group participated in four aspects of formative assessment. First, students helped define evaluation criteria. Second, they were taught how to apply the criteria to their own work. Third, they received feedback on the quality of their self-evaluations. Fourth, they used the results of their self-evaluations to develop plans for further learning. After controlling for prior knowledge (performance on a pretest), students with self-evaluation training outperformed those without on a math problem-solving task. The effect size was 0.40 standard deviations, or the equivalent of moving from the 50th percentile to the 66th percentile on a standardized test. The formative assessment process involves students in the learning process and gives them a measure of control over it.

Types of Data Available

Formative assessment methods vary widely, from informal classroom exercises and reflections to tests or quizzes that are used for formative purposes. Almost all formative assessment strategies fall into the following categories (Moss & Brookhart, 2009; Wiliam, 2010):

- Sharing learning targets and criteria for success with students
- Feedback that feeds forward, from teachers, peers, or other sources
- Student self-assessment and goal setting
- Using strategic questions and engaging students in asking effective questions

This book is not a primer on formative assessment strategies. Here I describe formative assessment strategies in just enough detail for you to see what the "results" look like. Consult other sources if you want a fuller treatment of the strategies (see, e.g., Moss & Brookhart, 2009; Wiliam, 2011).

Formative assessments yield a different kind of information from, say, that obtained from large-scale test scores, in at least four ways:

1. Classroom formative assessments assess learning outcomes at a small grain size because they are part of the flow of daily, lesson-by-lesson instruction.
2. Classroom formative assessment results are different for each student, because the student's involvement in the assessment and in taking next steps is part of the formative assessment process.
3. Classroom formative assessment results are usually based on teacher-made, and sometimes even student-generated, assessment items or tasks.
4. The primary users for classroom formative assessment results are students and their teachers.

The focus in this section is on how these characteristics of classroom formative assessment strategies affect the meaning of the data that the strategies yield.

Domain assessed

Classroom formative assessment strategies typically are used for taking a pulse on students' grasp of an immediate, lesson-sized chunk of content. These strategies are used "minute by minute, day by day" (Leahy, Lyon, Thompson, & Wiliam, 2005). Think about what sorts of things happen during classroom lessons and the grain size of learning targets for classroom lessons. Most formative assessment strategies give information about small bites of content, providing answers to questions such as these: "Can I put a period at the end of these simple sentences?" (not "Can I punctuate all declarative sentences properly?"). "Can I draw a cheek cell?" (not "What is my skill level at scientific drawing in general?"). "Can I explain why Leslie went to Terabithia without Jess that day?" (not "Can I explain how plot and characterization are related?").

Methods and results

Classroom formative assessment strategies are embedded within classroom instructional moves. The strategies are intended to yield evidence of student learning while that learning is taking place, and then be used to inform future steps for teachers and students as the learning moves forward. In this way, classroom formative assessment strategies support the formative assessment paradigm "Where am I going? Where am I now? Where should I go next?" (Hattie & Timperley, 2007; Sadler, 1989). Different authors have expressed formative assessment strategies for classroom teachers in slightly different ways, but they all express the ways by which classroom evidence-gathering for purposes of learning support the formative assessment paradigm.

Sharing learning targets and criteria for success with students. Sharing learning targets and criteria for success heads the list of formative assessment strategies, no matter how that list is constructed (Heritage, 2010; Moss & Brookhart, 2009; Wiliam, 2011). Formative assessment strategies should show students what it means to learn their lesson; the strategies do this by embodying the lesson's learning target. For example, if a lesson is focused on learning how to use vivid vocabulary in writing, the formative assessment should ask students to do just that—at the same time providing evidence of how well they do it and where they could improve, based on clear criteria (in this case, the criteria would identify what "using vivid vocabulary" looks like). The criteria for success enable students to get "evidence" from their work (e.g., "I use words that suggest pictures in my head; I use words that suggest smells, sounds, or tastes; I use words that suggest feelings"), see how well their work stacks up against the criteria, and internalize the criteria so they become part of the learning.

Feedback that feeds forward, from teachers, peers, or other sources. Like sharing learning targets, feedback—interpreting the evidence from student work according to how it matches the criteria and what should come next in the student's journey toward the learning target—is part of every list of formative assessment strategies (Heritage, 2010; Moss & Brookhart, 2009; Wiliam, 2011). Wiliam (2011) separates teacher feedback and peer feedback, which he calls "activating learners as instructional resources for one another" (p. 46).

Feedback comes as a response to various methods of eliciting evidence of student learning (Heritage, 2010; Wiliam, 2011). Those methods encompass a wide variety of techniques: single questions, classroom discussions, tasks (e.g., write a sentence, write a paragraph, draw a picture of what you see through the microscope), sets of questions (e.g., a quiz), exit tickets, and so on. For our discussion of "data," it is important to realize that the data that result from formative use of these and other evidence-eliciting strategies include both the correctness or quality of the student work *and the interpretation of that work as expressed in teacher, peer, or other feedback.*

Perhaps that point is best illustrated with a story. You can't tell by looking at an item whether it is part of a formative or a summative assessment. Here is a simple mathematics item that might be used in a classroom formative assessment, on a graded classroom test, on a benchmark assessment, or on an accountability assessment:

> Farmer Brown gets eggs from the henhouse every morning. Today he collected 636 eggs. He will sell them for $1.65 per dozen. How much money will he receive from the sale? Show your work.

The answer is $87.45, and student work should include dividing 636 by 12 in some way, using an algorithm or a diagram, to arrive at 53 dozen eggs, and multiplying 53 by $1.65, the price per dozen, in some way to arrive at a total price of $87.45.

On a classroom test, this item might be marked right or wrong, or it might be marked with a math problem-solving rubric. On an interim assessment or an accountability assessment, the item might be scored either of those ways and then scaled using a mathematical model such as item response theory. When formative assessment is well done, however, the score is not the primary information this item would yield. The feedback and information for what to do next is the primary assessment information. Consider a class where the teacher gave this question, then asked students to solve it and discuss their work in groups. One student might have gotten a wrong answer and say, "I can do this problem. I just put the decimal point in the wrong place after I multiplied. I should be more careful about that." Another student might have gotten a wrong answer and say, "I had trouble figuring out where in the problem I needed to divide and where to multiply. I should work on deciding when to multiply and when to divide." These are two different insights, two different pieces of data about student learning, from the same incorrectly worked problem.

Student self-assessment and goal setting. Formative assessment strategies also include student self-assessment and goal setting (Moss & Brookhart, 2009), variously expressed as scaffolding new learning and closing the gap (Heritage, 2010) or activating learners as the owners of their own learning (Wiliam, 2011).

The data that come from student self-assessment and goal setting are in the form of feedback to oneself—an appraisal of "where I am" with regard to the learning target I'm attempting and what I should study or include in my work next—and goals and action plans based on my appraisal of my own learning. In other words, these appraisals and goal statements are "data" because they are reasoned interpretations of evidence of student learning and achievement, but they are not numbers. Nevertheless, they tell us a lot about student learning.

Using strategic questions and engaging students in asking effective questions. This category of formative assessment evidence is a special case of general methods to elicit evidence of student learning. I pull it out here because of the special importance of the quality and nature of questions for formative assessment (Moss & Brookhart, 2009; Wiliam, 2011). Questions that elicit student thinking and make students verbalize it—either orally or in writing—get that thinking outside of kids' heads and into public space where teachers and classmates can hear it, assess it, and respond to it. Strategic questions that require thinking about a learning target of interest, as opposed to right/wrong questions that ascertain whether students can recall certain facts, help both students and teachers turn student thoughts into evidence of learning. Helping students learn to ask effective questions—questions that show what they are thinking about a particular concept—also helps turn student thoughts into evidence of learning.

The "data" in these cases are the questions themselves—what students want to know—and also appraisals, against criteria, of the depth and quality of student thinking about the concepts and skills they are trying to learn. Again, these data are not numbers, but they are powerful evidence about student learning that can be leveraged to improve future learning.

Aggregation

The primary "data" from classroom formative assessments, as we have seen, are qualitative appraisals of quality of thought and insights about next steps to take in learning. As we saw in the story about the Farmer Brown item, different kinds of information may come from the same item or task "score." This is why classroom formative assessment results are not able to be aggregated, even when a whole class does the same item. (How would you aggregate the two students' insights, one about a careless error and the other about the concepts of division and multiplication?) A teacher might want to know what proportion of the class got the item correct, or the general level of problem solving on a rubric, but that is not the assessment information that gives traction to student learning. In other words, the score is not what is formative.

Use of information

The primary use of formative assessment results is for students to take those immediate next steps in learning that will move them along their learning trajectory from today's lesson to tomorrow's, and ultimately help them achieve their intended curricular goals and state standards. In this way, teachers and students, together, are the primary users of information.

Classroom formative assessment information can play a role in the interpretation of large-scale assessment information, when it is used to put "meat on the bones" of the broad generalizations that large-scale information supports. It is particularly useful in this regard for decisions about individuals. For example, if one of your students had disappointing results on the state reading test, you might find clues about what, specifically, he had trouble with when you think back over the progression of his classroom formative work. Was it vocabulary? Finding the main idea? Making inferences when ideas were particularly abstract?

What You Can (and Can't) Learn from Classroom Formative Assessment Data

The good news about the tiny packets of information available from formative assessment results is that they are the most instructionally actionable of all assessment data about student learning. Formative assessments usually yield student work to refer to and feedback on that work by the teacher, the student himself, or peers. This detailed, albeit narrow, set of information ideally shows the student and the teacher something that the student did well and something that should happen next, and thus places itself squarely into an instructional sequence.

Without further data, you can't generalize from one small piece of day-to-day formative assessment information to a larger domain. If formative assessment is doing its job, student learning should change. But even if learning doesn't change, a small slice of a larger domain of content is not a good basis on which to generalize. However, you can look to formative assessment information, especially if you look at a series of formative assessment information over time, as corroboration and illustration—or sometimes contradiction—of patterns that you have observed in assessments of larger domains of knowledge. For example, if a unit test suggested that a student couldn't identify character traits that helped drive plot, you could look to daily formative assessment results to try to figure out why.

The very best use of classroom formative assessment results happens when the teacher uses evidence of individual students' thinking to adjust something (or to conclude that no adjustment is needed), usually feedback to the student or future instruction, and when the student uses evidence of his or her progress toward a learning target to take another step forward, usually by focusing study or revising work. The next sections continue our running examples, where, as you know, the focus is making broader, school-wide decisions. Classroom formative assessment information has some use in this regard, as you'll see. As you read the following examples, though, keep in mind that the primary use of this information would have already happened during daily lessons (Moss & Brookhart, 2009; Wiliam, 2011).

Example—School 1

You will recall that the educators at School 1 had looked at students' grades and what kind of work was graded. In mathematics, students were required to show and explain their work, in the process using multiple representations of mathematical thinking, metacognitive skills, and mathematical communication skills. These skills, along with computation and problem solving, matched the state standards and state assessment. In contrast, in reading, students were mostly required to demonstrate literal and inferential comprehension. These skills were only a partial match with the state standards and state assessment. These observations had led the educators in School 1 to a tentative hypothesis: *Our students are doing OK with the curriculum as we teach it, but in mathematics students have to think more deeply than in reading, and this effort matches better with the state standards.* To support or refute this tentative hypothesis, they needed evidence about what the students actually *were* thinking as they did their work. Classroom formative assessment is the best place to look for that.

However, in reading they found little evidence of formative assessment taking place. They did find classroom learning activities and student work to look at, but there was no evidence the work had been used for formative assessment. For example, in 8th grade reading, students had read an article about artist Georgia O'Keeffe. Then, in class, they were asked to make a time line of events in the artist's life as described in the passage. This was a comprehension-level activity. An examination of most of the students' time lines showed that they listed the dates in the article in chronological order and then copied sentences or phrases out of the reading next to the appropriate date. Because most of the students did the task this way, it was reasonable to conclude that they saw the task as reproducing correct facts from the text. There was no evidence that students had reflected on the meaning or importance of the events they had read about. A 7th grade reading activity involved reading a passage about the explorer Marco Polo and using information from the passage to draw on a map the route Marco Polo had taken in the excerpt

they read. The map work was carefully done and had been marked with a check, a plus, or a minus sign.

In contrast, in mathematics students had been using a rubric with three criteria: Mathematical Knowledge, Problem Solving Strategies, and Mathematical Communication. As students did problem sets in class, they explained their work and then applied these rubrics to see where they were in relation to the standard. One student wrote, on the rubrics stapled to one of the problem sets about ratios, "It's much easier for me to write what I did than why I did it. I should practice looking for reasons." Another student wrote, "I got the right answer, but I guessed at how to solve the problem. That made it hard to explain my work." And another, explaining her work on solving equations with one variable, wrote, "I knew when I ended up dividing by zero that I had done something wrong."

In all, looking over student work—and especially the results of formative assessment— corroborated the hypothesis that reading was taught mostly as literal and inferential comprehension. In mathematics, students had an opportunity to explain their work and reflect on it, and their reflections indicated that many of them were able to think behind what they were doing to the reasons why they were doing it. For a small group of students, reflections and use of the rubrics suggested they were not able to explain their work very well. Those same students had mostly scored in the Not Proficient range on the state test.

Example—School 2

In School 2, teachers found that most of the day-to-day work students had done in mathematics, which could have been used for formative purposes, was in the form of exercises exactly like the ones on the unit tests. The exercises were not particularly difficult, but they did afford practice at applying the algorithm students were learning in the particular unit. Math classroom work was mostly drill of the "plug and chug" variety. Most students didn't write anything on their math classwork except computations and answers. Teacher feedback mostly consisted of marking things right or wrong. On classwork papers with a lot marked wrong, teachers sometimes wrote "See me."

Some classroom formative assessment opportunities in a few lessons happened near the end of a unit, when students were given review sheets that did not include solely one type of problem. Student performance on these was not as high as for the unified practice sheets and the unit tests. The review sheets did not seem to be used for formative purposes—there was no feedback on them. They were more like an activity rather than an assessment, without apparent follow-up on the results. The actual student work on these problems showed that when students were correct, they followed the algorithm that had been taught for that type of problem. When they were incorrect, their work stalled in the middle of the problem as they forgot what to do next.

Concluding Thoughts

In these examples, I have tried to illustrate the finer-grain-size observations that can be made by looking at student formative assessment work—usually classroom work and reflections upon it. There are other kinds of formative assessment information—for example, from student and teacher use of oral questions. For these you need classroom observations because they don't leave a paper or artifact trail. It is only when you see what kind of thinking the students are actually doing that you have enough information to plan whether you should design changes in curriculum or instruction, and if so, what those might be. We turn to a discussion of those plans in Chapter 6.

It may seem depressing to look at student work and come up with so many negative observations. That's because in both of our examples, teachers in a school were looking to explain why student work was not as proficient as desired. In my experience, those are the sorts of follow-up questions that are most likely to be asked: What are we doing poorly, and how can we improve it? That's why I chose these particular examples. It is possible to use data to make decisions about the need for enrichment and extension, and I promise you'll find one of those examples in the next chapter.

Putting It All Together: Basing Decisions on Data

	More Large Scale	
INTERIM/BENCHMARK Assessments **COMMON** Formative Assessments	**ACCOUNTABILITY** Assessments (School, District, State, National, International)	

More Formative Purpose ←

Classroom **FORMATIVE ASSESSMENT** Strategies	**GRADING** Classroom Summative Assessments, Report Card Grades

→ More Summative Purpose

More Classroom Focused

No educational decision should jump right from data to a plan or a solution. Information simply exists, and it requires interpretation. This reality is easiest to see in a simple example. Suppose you have two students in your class, Hailey and Brayden, who are not doing their math homework. That's your observation—your data. If you reasoned directly from the data (no homework) to the solution, you would probably do something like keep the students in from recess and make them do their homework. This kind of reasoning says that the data *are* (did you know the word *data* is plural?) the problem. No homework; therefore, make them do homework.

But data are neutral. They are not problems, even problems in the sense of conundrums or issues to address, which is how I am using the word in this chapter. Data are *indicators* or *symptoms* of something. You have to reason from the data to the "something," the issue or problem, before you can solve it.

So let's return to the data: Hailey and Brayden are not doing their homework. To identify the problem, you need to find out why. After talking with both students, you find out that Hailey lives with her mother and grandmother plus quite a few other family members in an apartment where there is a lot of noise and very little space. There is no place for her to do her homework, and when she is at home she has other things to concentrate on. You find out that Brayden often doesn't understand his homework, and he'd rather not do it than do it "wrong."

These are two different problems, and they require two different solutions. You might try, as your first plan of action, working with Hailey and her mother to figure out a way she can do her homework at home. Your first plan of action for Brayden might be to differentiate instruction for him during math class, working with him and several others in smaller steps and giving smaller, more scaffolded homework assignments. If you had simply reasoned from the data to a solution, you would have missed the mark and been less than effective with both students.

Because of the weight that state tests carry, it can be very tempting to reason from state test scores and jump to a "solution." Consider this example: Math scores are down; therefore, we should increase instructional time for math and make students work harder. This error is the same error as reasoning from no homework to staying in at recess; it's just harder to see. This kind of rush to judgment assumes the data (low math scores) *are* the problem. They are not. The data are indicators or symptoms of something, and you need to find out what.

Querying Your Data

The way we approached identifying the underlying problem in our examples was to use questions. First, ask a question of your data (e.g., How have students performed over the last four years in math?) and organize it to get the answer (e.g., Performance has risen slightly but is still lower than we would like.). You will remember that's how we made our first graphs of state test data in Chapter 2. Then use the data display to ask "why" and other questions that will help you identify the underlying problem. Don't limit yourself only to questions about student achievement. At this stage it's important to ask about the nature of instruction, the classroom environment, and anything else you think might be relevant.

Answering complex questions and making decisions about what to do next require data of more than one type. Figure out what kind of data you need for your purpose. If your data include state test data, you will usually want to find out how students have been doing on more local measures. Our four-quadrant framework should help you identify good sources of achievement data that are closer to the learning because it will show you four different places to look. You will also usually want to find out what your curriculum intended for students to learn, how that played out in the classroom, and how all of that aligned with the state standards and the state test. What kinds of instruction and activities have students experienced? That is, what has been the nature of the "taught curriculum"? Does the classroom environment support student thinking, questioning, and active learning, or is it more set up for students to produce "right answers"?

Identifying the Problem

Gather more data to answer your "why" questions. Use different kinds of data as multiple measures that work together to tell a story about learning. For example, to find out why math achievement has risen slightly but is still lower than we would like, look at the work students have been doing. Look at the scores or results on that work and also at evidence of the nature of student mathematical thinking and teacher feedback. Look at the lessons teachers have been teaching. What concepts and skills have been stressed? What has been their approach to teaching mathematics? Has instruction aligned with all, part, or none of the standards? You will be mixing data about student achievement—the kinds of data in the four-quadrant framework—with teacher observations and judgments about curriculum, instruction, and student thinking.

Then, when you think you have figured out what the problem is, identify it. I mean that literally: articulate the problem in words, in writing. Write a few sentences that summarize what you think the foundational issue, root cause, or essential problem is. You can't solve a problem until you know what it is. Articulating the problem will help make sure that everyone understands exactly what the issue is.

Working Together to Use Data to Change Schoolwide or Subjectwide Instruction

Teacher observations and judgments are often collected during facilitated meeting times. Some schools have data-review teams who do this. Other schools use time at faculty meetings or professional learning team sessions. Data teams may do the initial query of the data and data display, constructing graphs that will focus teacher discussion on particular comparisons of interest. Then they can construct a protocol for teachers to use to come to consensus on identifying the problem (first) and planning a tentative solution (second).

I can't stress enough the importance of having a facilitated discussion and using a protocol to work through the problem-solving process. It's easy to get off track when discussing classroom instruction and student learning. It's easy to get off on tangents that are either about blame—for example, blaming some teachers or students for doing something "wrong"—or about things we can't control—numbers of students or socioeconomic issues, for example. Educational decisions that bring about improvement must be based on focused discussion about teaching and learning, based on evidence. Using a skilled facilitator and implementing a protocol are both methods for keeping the discussion focused. Figure 6.1 gives an example of a two-part protocol to support identifying the problem and planning a tentative solution.

Once the problem is articulated, use a *logic model* to construct a path from an understanding of the problem to a potential solution. A logic model is a tool borrowed from the field of program evaluation. Logic models are usually diagrammed and often look like simple flow charts. The logic model depicts hypothesized cause-and-effect relationships among elements in the educational program. Some examples are shown in the next section. Of course, the important part is that the reasoning must be logical so that the action plan—what you are going to do about the problem you have identified—is reasonable.

You could just write all this down in notes. The diagram is a nice tool, however, because it forces you to "fill in the boxes": a box for what the problem is, a box for your tentative solution, and one or more boxes for

---

FIGURE 6.1

Example of a Protocol for a Data Discussion Session

Preparation: A data team has selected the data to review and has done an initial analysis. This analysis involved posing a question to the data with an implied comparison (e.g., How do this year's state test reading scores compare with last year's scores? or What progress do students' scores on a benchmark test show across three administrations during the year?) and making a graph or chart that highlights that comparison. The data team has also brought information from other relevant sources, for example, assessment data from other quadrants in the four-quadrant framework.

A facilitator is assigned or selected. A recorder takes notes. The following protocol may take one meeting or several, depending on whether time is needed to collect and organize additional data.

1. Presentation. The data team presents the data it has reviewed and its initial analysis, highlighting the important comparison. Participants review the data presented, listen, and take notes.

2. Initial discussion and identification of a student performance pattern. Participants have a discussion based on these questions. [Note: The student performance pattern is not the "problem." Problem identification comes in step 4.]

- What pattern(s) do we see in the student performance data? Participants frame the pattern as a pattern with "student" as the subject of the sentence, for example, "Sixth grade students are scoring too low in Mathematics" or "Low-SES students achieve proficiency in Reading at significantly lower rates than other students."
- What might be some reasons for these patterns? Participants list all possible reasons, in the style of a brainstorming session.

3. Identification of additional data. Participants identify additional data in order to hypothesize a reason for the student performance pattern that is amenable to intervention.

- Where can we get additional data about student learning that will help us identify the most likely reasons for the pattern? Who will locate the data and bring them to us (if the data team has not already done so)?
- Where can we get additional data about classroom instruction that will help us identify the most likely reasons for the pattern? Who will locate the data and bring them to us (if the data team has not already done so)?

(continued)

FIGURE 6.1

Example of a Protocol for a Data Discussion Session *(continued)*

4. Review of additional data and identification of a problem to solve. Participants review additional data and have a discussion based on these questions. Flip charts and sticky notes may be used to collect and group comments, especially if the group is large.

- What kind of work were students asked to do? How well do these assignments/assessments match content area standards? What patterns were observable in student performance on these assignments/assessments?
- What do the additional sources of data suggest are the reasons for the pattern(s) we observed in our original data?
- Of all the reasons identified in Step 2, which ones are supported as the most likely by the additional data? Participants articulate the problem in one or two sentences that begin with something the school can control (e.g., instruction, materials, curriculum). For example, "Mathematics instruction too often emphasizes rote application of procedures."

[Take stock at this point and decide whether to continue or to end the session here and start a future session with step 5.]

5. Planning a tentative solution. Based on the problem identified in step 4, participants hypothesize what solutions might be effective. What changes might be made in instruction, assessment, and/or curriculum to address and potentially ameliorate the problem? Again, flip charts and sticky notes may be used to collect and group comments, especially if the group is large.

6. Constructing a logic model. Participants construct a logic model. State the problem (from step 4) in the first box, leading to the tentative solution(s) in the next box or boxes. In the following box or boxes, state what you expect will happen if the tentative solution is implemented. In the final box or boxes, identify data you will be able to collect to evaluate the effectiveness of your solution. Check that the progression from box to box is logical.

7. Debriefing and next steps. The facilitator leads the participants in a discussion of how satisfied they are with the problem identification, tentative solution, and logic model they have created. The group decides on next steps for implementing the solution. For example, if the logic model specified math teachers will make some instructional changes, the group that will be doing that planning decides how to do it and when to meet. The session should end with the participants having a clear idea of how the tentative solution will be implemented, who is responsible, and what data will be collected to evaluate progress.

hypothesized effects, which you can then evaluate. When plans are not diagrammed in a logic model, you risk not having a clear path from a statement
of the problem to intended, measurable effects.

This chapter's examples focus on reasoning from data to identify the
problem and pose a tentative solution. These solutions are usually the "decisions" people have in mind when they use the phrase "data-based decision
making." The decisions themselves, however, should generate data that we
can use to see if our decisions led in an effective manner to the improvements we were hoping for. Chapter 7 will focus on evaluating the results of
the decisions.

The cases of School 1 and School 2 have been our running examples,
which began with considering state test scores. At this point, both schools
have a tentative hypothesis about how learning in their school could be
improved. Although the state test scores served as a catalyst for asking follow-
up questions and doing some detective work about student learning, most of
the information that was useful for identifying the problem came from a look
at students' classroom work and teachers' classroom instruction. Let's look
at how, in each school, educators' reasoning based on state test scores led to
changes in subjectwide or schoolwide instruction.

Example—School 1

Educators in School 1 had decided that the reason reading achievement
was lower overall than they would like was that the curriculum, at least as
taught in reading classes, covered only part of the state's reading standards.
Reading instruction and assessment maintained a narrow focus on literal and
inferential comprehension. Issues of writer's purpose and audience were not
addressed. Neither was making connections between and among texts. The
reading teachers decided to make some changes in curriculum and instruction to see if they could broaden and deepen the reading curriculum while
still maintaining an appropriate level of emphasis on comprehension. They
believed their problem was systemic, that the lack of achievement was not just
because of narrowly focused teaching but because all of the standards were
not addressed in the curriculum.

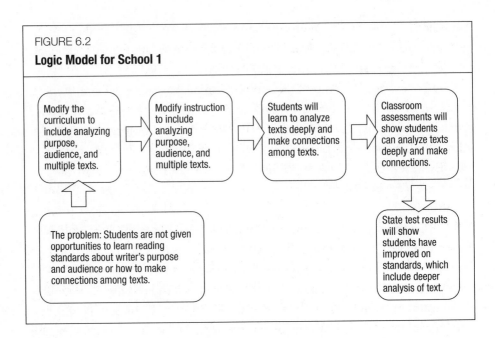

FIGURE 6.2

Logic Model for School 1

Modify the curriculum to include analyzing purpose, audience, and multiple texts.

Modify instruction to include analyzing purpose, audience, and multiple texts.

Students will learn to analyze texts deeply and make connections among texts.

Classroom assessments will show students can analyze texts deeply and make connections.

The problem: Students are not given opportunities to learn reading standards about writer's purpose and audience or how to make connections among texts.

State test results will show students have improved on standards, which include deeper analysis of text.

The reading teachers in School 1 built the logic model shown in Figure 6.2. Note that the direction of the arrows and the logic of cause and effect are the important features of the model. The boxes could be all in one line reading left to right. The bend in this diagram is simply for convenience of display. The diagram is a tool that reflects teachers' reasoning from a problem through a two-step solution, modifying both curriculum and classroom instruction, to an effect on student learning that can be evaluated with two different measures: classroom and large-scale assessments. As the next school year progresses, the teachers in School 1 may also decide to collect additional information—for example, from observing or talking with students about their work or talking with colleagues about their instruction.

Example—School 2

The teachers in School 2 identified a different problem. They hypothesized that the reason for low math achievement was lack of opportunity for students to learn problem solving and mathematical thinking in class. These aspects of the standards were present in the curriculum, but in most classes teachers had been interpreting "problem solving" to mean "doing math problems" as exemplified in the conventional, single-method, one-right-answer problem sets they had been using. Their tentative solution, then, was not to change the curriculum but to increase classroom instruction in problem solving and mathematical thinking. The hypothesized effect would be increased student learning in those areas, indicated by two kinds of measurable outcomes: higher scores on classroom assessments and large-scale tests. Figure 6.3 shows the logic model for School 2. As for School 1, the tentative solution is based on the answers to the "why" questions asked about the state test scores and the answers found from looking at additional data from examinations of student work and classroom instruction.

As with School 1, the logic model makes it easy to see what to do. That doesn't necessarily mean it will be easy to actually do it, though. Do teachers know how to do mathematics instruction differently to foster mathematical thinking? If not, some professional development may be in order. Major shifts

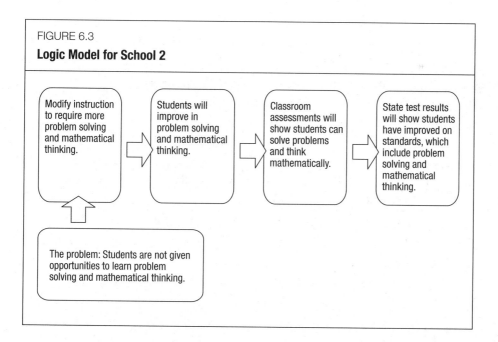

FIGURE 6.3

Logic Model for School 2

Modify instruction to require more problem solving and mathematical thinking.

Students will improve in problem solving and mathematical thinking.

Classroom assessments will show students can solve problems and think mathematically.

State test results will show students have improved on standards, which include problem solving and mathematical thinking.

The problem: Students are not given opportunities to learn problem solving and mathematical thinking.

in instruction don't come easily for teachers or for students. But the logic model, at least, presents the road map.

Teachers Using Data to Change Classroom Instruction

In addition to schoolwide or subjectwide issues, classroom-level issues involve individual teachers in examining data and using them to make informed decisions about possible changes in their instruction. Two obvious sources of such data are grades and classroom formative assessment.

Student grades

Have you ever had disappointing performance from your students after a unit of instruction, as shown by a grade distribution you didn't like? More *F*s than you wanted, for example, or more students than you expected not reaching proficiency? This experience happens to almost all teachers at least once in a while. Instead of just moving on to the next unit, glad that this one is over, try treating those grades as the "data" from which to start the data-based decision-making process.

Just as with our large-scale examples, first query the data. Did everyone achieve below your expectations for them, or was it just a certain group—and if so, what are the characteristics of this group as learners? Once you have a better idea of performance, ask your follow-up questions: Why did everyone, or why did a certain group, not reach the unit's learning goals? What did their classroom formative assessment (practice) work look like? Did they use that information formatively? Did you? Can you tell by looking at the work what the students were thinking? What concepts or skills did they have the most trouble with? Were they beginning to get it when time ran out, or were they confused throughout the unit? Ask the appropriate questions, and then use your answers to draw up an informal logic model to do something about it.

For example, if a social studies teacher found students made too many errors of fact on a unit test but did a nice job in class discussions and on a project that required original research and a class presentation, her tentative hypothesis might be that students did not study efficiently. She might plan to address that issue in the next unit, helping students set up study plans and study buddies. However, if she found that the content of students' discussions and written work showed misunderstandings about concepts from the unit—for example, misconceptions about the principles of democracy as articulated in the Preamble to the U.S. Constitution—her tentative hypothesis might be that all or some students did not understand vital content. Accordingly, she might plan not to go on to the next unit immediately, but to take a day or two to reteach the whole class. Or she might decide to go on to the next unit and identify a small group to pull aside for additional assistance during classroom work time.

These instructional modifications would lead to more data in the form of student work that the teacher could use to evaluate the effectiveness of her data-based decision making. A major point here is that data-based decision making does not have to be based on large-scale assessment results. Teachers can use the process of reasoning from data in the classroom. The same principle we have seen for approaching large-scale data holds for within-classroom use of data: Do *not* jump from the data to a solution. That is, "too many *F*s" is not the problem. It's a symptom or an indicator of the problem. Ask follow-up questions about the reasons for the pattern in the data. Look at more data, including observations of student work, and draw your conclusions from this broader picture. Once you have identified a problem, you can propose a tentative solution, carry it out, and evaluate its effects.

Classroom formative assessment

For day-to-day classroom formative assessment, the data comprise observations by both students and teachers. This example will be the positive example promised at the end of the previous chapter. In this case, the "problem" is that a student reaches the learning target quickly and without difficulty and needs some direction about what to do next. This example also differs from our previous examples in having a very short cycle and focusing on a very small aspect of content knowledge and skill. However, it follows the same process for data-based decision making as we have applied to larger-scale problems. Finally, notice that this example also involves the student. If you look back at Figure 1.2 (p. 12), you will find that this example demonstrates what should be the *most frequent* and *most important* use of assessment information: improving learning while it happens, using classroom formative assessment.

A 2nd grade teacher is introducing fractions to her students. They have learned that fractions name parts of a region. Their previous lesson was about unit fractions (e.g., 1/2, 1/3), and they spent the lesson learning to write unit fractions to describe shapes that had been divided into equal parts and had one of the parts shaded. Today the teacher tells students they will be learning to write more fractions. This time, they will have to count the number of shaded parts, because there could be more than one. The student look-fors for today's learning target are presented to the students as questions to ask themselves as they work:

- Do I have a line between my top and bottom numbers?
- Did I write the number of shaded parts above the line?
- Did I write the total number of parts below the line?
- Can I explain why this fraction describes the picture?

The teacher begins by modeling with the whole class how to write a fraction for each illustration. For example, a circle divided into three equal parts, with two shaded, would be represented by 2/3. The teacher shows how 2/3 is a good way to represent the picture because it says that "two out of three parts" are selected, and that matches the picture. Then she gives students pictures of different shapes that are equally divided into parts, with guided questions such as "How many parts are yellow?" and "How many total equal parts are there?" Students are to answer the questions and then write the fraction. Students are to use the look-fors to check their work.

The teacher circulates as the students are working and gives feedback. Most of her feedback involves using the look-for questions with students to focus them on noticing and understanding their own work. In the class, three students work quickly, neatly, and accurately, finishing well before the rest of the class. This observation is the "data" the teacher starts with: these three students finished quickly and accurately. She asks the students about their work, and they can tell her what they learned. They have self-assessed using the look-fors she gave the class. They know what they know.

To gather more information about why—checking that her interpretation of these students' accomplishment is sound and at the same time giving them the opportunity to extend their learning—she asks each one some extension questions. These questions would be designed to make students think and also to gather information about the quality of their thinking and depth of understanding. For example, Can you think of a fraction that would be smaller than this one (pointing to the 2/3 shaded shape)? How would you know? Would your new fraction have the same top number? Would it have the same bottom number? Why?

These extension questions don't take any longer than the feedback the teacher gives to other students who are still working. They are a seamless part of her instruction. The students' explanations for their answers demonstrate that they have learned the intended content for the lesson. There are still 10 minutes left in the class, and more important, the three students are motivated to proceed. They know that they can do this work. They are ready to learn more. The teacher makes a decision to deepen their learning in this same content area, based on the standard she is teaching (about understanding fractions and being able to use them to solve problems). She gives the students two questions to work on. First, she asks them to draw their own shape, divide it into equal parts, shade some of the parts, and write the fraction they have just diagrammed. She asks them to try to make it a different shape or with a different number of parts than in the problems they just did. Then she poses them a challenge: If you can, draw something "real" (like a pizza or a sandwich or a garden plot)—not just a shape—that you could divide into equal parts. Shade some of the parts, write the fraction, and tell a story about your fraction.

These extra questions would not be graded; they are for formative assessment and extending learning. Assigning these questions was the "decision" the teacher made. Her logic model was informal and inside her head, but it ran something like this: *These three students understand how to represent fractions as parts of a whole, both with diagrams and numbers. They need to stay challenged. They are ready to deepen their knowledge on this same standard. If I pose questions that are more difficult and require problem solving, they will stay challenged and learn to solve problems with fractions.* This is her tentative hypothesis. She will soon have the data to evaluate the effectiveness of her decision. These data will come in two forms: the teacher's observation of the students' work on the challenge questions, and the students' own self-assessments about what they have learned.

Students Using Data from Classroom Formative Assessment to Change Learning

Finally, the aspect of classroom formative assessment that sets it apart from business as usual in the classroom is the involvement of students in their own learning (Andrade, 2010; Wiliam, 2010). Formative assessment empowers students to participate in the cycle marked by three questions: Where am I going? Where am I now? How can I close the gap? (Hattie & Timperley, 2007; Sadler, 1989). The formative learning cycle relies on data. The first data point for a formative learning cycle is the student's understanding of her learning target (Where am I going?). What is it she is supposed to learn, and what will it look like when she does? This concept of the learning target should come with criteria, or student look-fors, that will help the student assess her own work. Information about a student's current knowledge and skills (Where am I now?) comes from self-assessment, teacher feedback, and sometimes peer assessment against the criteria. Information about what to do next (How can I close the gap?), similarly, comes from self-assessment, teacher feedback, and sometimes peer assessment.

Teach students to use the formative assessment process as a routine part of their learning. You will be, in effect, supporting a short-cycle, limited-perspective, but nonetheless data-based decision-making process for students. For example, a student might do a draft of an informational essay about how to raise a puppy and read it against a set of criteria, one of which might be about organization. He might realize he does not have an organizational scheme in his essay and work to improve that, imposing an organizational scheme based on topic (feeding, potty training, exercising, socializing) for the next draft. Although students' formative, data-based decision making will not result in graphs or logic models, it should nonetheless be logical and supported by evidence.

Concluding Thoughts

At this point it is possible to summarize the process for data-based decision making. We haven't come to the end of it yet—evaluating results is still to come in Chapter 7—but I have described enough of the process to sensibly summarize it. To make sense of data, remember that data (e.g., low test scores) are *not* the problem. They are a symptom or an indicator of something. Once you understand that, you can take the following five steps:

1. Reason from data, via follow-up questioning and inspecting additional data, to a statement of a problem. Remember that a "problem" is simply a conundrum to solve; it may not be a bad thing.
2. Then reason from your statement of the problem to a tentative solution. This is the "decision" in the term "data-based decision making." This reasoning should be stated in a logic model that uses cause-and-effect reasoning to posit intended outcomes. For decisions that begin with schoolwide, large-scale assessment data, the logic model should be written down and diagrammed. For short-term classroom decisions in real time, the logic model will be in your head, but it should nonetheless be reasonable and based on evidence.
3. Try out the tentative solution. This might be a change in policy, a change in curriculum or instruction, or a classroom adaptation for one or a few students.
4. Evaluate the effectiveness of your solution by looking at intended outcomes and any other relevant information—for example, teacher or student observations.

5. Use your results to start the data-driven decision-making cycle all over again. If the solution was effective, build on it by starting from the new data and using the process to make another decision. If it was not effective, try to figure out why, using the data-based decision-making process. In either case, literally go back to "square one," or Step 1 in this summary list.

Chapters 2 through 5 discussed reasoning from data (Step 1). In this chapter, we have considered planning and acting on the decisions that resulted after reasoning from data (Steps 2 and 3). In the next chapter, we'll discuss evaluating the effectiveness of your tentative solution (Step 4). Step 5 reminds us that the process is cyclical, as are all educational action research initiatives (Noffke & Somekh, 2009). One good decision is terrific, but it's only one step in the ongoing process of helping all your students learn all they can.

But Did They Learn Anything?
Evaluating the Results of Your Decisions

7

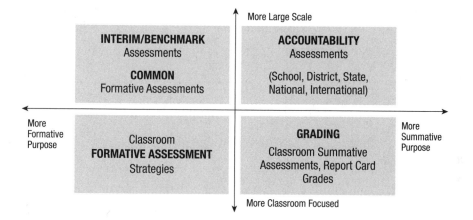

The final step in any data-based decision-making process is to evaluate the results of your decisions and modify them as necessary. The whole process is a cycle. It's not—or, at least, shouldn't be—limited to one decision. Modifying curriculum and instruction and finding out how students are learning is a central process in a school.

Data-based decision making, then, is the whole process, from querying data to gathering more data, identifying a problem, reasoning from the problem to a solution, trying out the solution, and evaluating it (Boudett et al., 2013; James-Ward et al., 2013). Data-based decision making is actually a special case of the more generalized, practice-based research process known as action research (Noffke & Somekh, 2009). For more than half a century, educators have known that addressing educational problems with an inquiry method is a reasonable, productive, and effective strategy for improvement in both teaching and learning. I think the current climate, with its emphasis on data in general and test results in particular, has made data-based decision making seem like something new and trendy, but it really isn't. It may be simply an idea whose time has come.

How to Decide What Data You Need to Monitor the Results of Your Decisions

The data you need to monitor the results of your decisions depend on what your decision was intended to accomplish. In this book, I have been focusing on decisions intended to improve student learning and achievement. The focus on decisions about student learning has been intentional, and the four-quadrant framework has been used to describe types of data for assessing student learning. This chapter highlights ways to monitor the effects of educational decisions on student learning outcomes, but before we do that, I want to remind you that there are other kinds of data. Decisions about teaching and learning are not the only kind of educational decisions. Other purposes for educational decisions include, for example, improving classroom environments, giving more ownership of learning to students, improving administrative efficiency for some task, improving graduation rates, increasing home-school communication, and improving attendance. The process just described (query your data, identify a problem, pose a tentative solution, try out the solution, evaluate its effectiveness, then begin the cycle again) works for all kinds of data-based decision making.

Deciding on measures

Understanding that our focus is on decisions intended to improve student learning, we can proceed to answer the question about how to decide what data you need in order to monitor and evaluate the results of a decision. The process you used to reason from some data to an underlying problem and a hypothesized solution, as we saw in Chapter 6, should include hypothesized effects. Part of deciding what you are going to do is determining what impact you want to have. If you have used a logic model, at least one of the boxes should include a measurable outcome, as in the examples of Schools 1 and 2 in the previous chapter. Classroom decisions should be logical, even if they don't use a formal logic model. In the classroom-level examples in the previous chapter, intended outcomes were held in mind or stated verbally between teacher and students, but they still included the intention that student work would be of higher quality and give evidence of intended learning.

The four-quadrant framework can help in deciding what measure to use to evaluate the results of changes in curriculum, instruction, or student involvement in learning. Recall that in Chapters 2 through 5 I described how measures in each of the four quadrants describe learning at different grain sizes. Large-scale accountability assessments measure large domains of achievement—for example, all priority mathematics standards for a certain grade level. Interim/benchmark assessments can measure at a slightly smaller grain size—for example, Algebraic Concepts—although they often measure only general achievement in a very similar manner to state tests. Assessments closer to the classroom measure smaller learning domains and give more detailed information about exactly what students learned. Report card grades measure a set of learning outcomes taught during a report period. Individual tests and performance assessments—classroom graded work—measure student performance on a smaller set of learning outcomes, often, for example, a set of unit goals. Classroom formative assessment information concerns the smallest grain size of information and can give information about student learning at the level of one lesson's learning target.

When you change curriculum or instruction, it is wise to look at effects using several different measures from different quadrants. You may, like School 1, make some changes in reading curriculum and instruction with the long-term hope of increasing large-scale accountability results. But with a broad domain, such as "reading," any one accountability test may include only a handful of questions that are directly related to the changes you made, and it may be difficult to register an effect on such a broad measure, at least right away. Some people use the metaphor "turning the battleship" to describe effects of school-level and district-level changes in curriculum and instruction on large-scale tests. More focused measures—the skiffs and motorboats, if you will—can turn faster. That's because, on a classroom test or even a common formative assessment, you can concentrate on measuring learning that is directly relevant to the changes you made. School 1, for example, might ask students to write essays comparing two texts to see how well students had learned that particular standard. This is why the logic models for School 1 and School 2 included two kinds of outcome data: classroom assessments and state assessments. One would expect classroom data to change before state data do: skiffs turn faster than battleships.

Deciding on the unit of analysis

Unit of analysis means the entity you are studying. Are you interested, as School 1 is, in the overall performance of all students in your school? Are you interested, as School 2 is, in the overall performance of students in each grade? Are you interested in the overall performance of students in a particular class, or certain groups of students, or the performance of individuals? Match your unit of analysis to the instructional decision you made. Was the decision about instruction for all students, certain groups of students, or individuals?

The decision you make about your unit of analysis will help you determine what sort of analysis you need to do. If you want to know about the performance of an individual student, you will need individual assessment results. These could be individual scores or grades or detailed descriptions of students' work. If you want to know about the performance of a group, you need aggregated measures. If you want to know about changes, you need comparable before-and-after data. If you are thinking "Didn't we read something about this before?" you are right! Different kinds of data, as described in Chapters 2 through 5, should be treated differently. We have already seen the perils of using changes in percent-proficient to describe changes in learning.

I'm going to describe some defensible ways of looking at change for individuals and groups. There are many other ways, including some very sophisticated analyses that require special software. I am assuming that you are interested in ways that you can evaluate the effects of educational decisions within a classroom, school, or district and present results to colleagues in ways they can understand. The purpose of these evaluations is to further the data-based decision-making process. So the goal here is to understand what you can and can't do with different kinds of data to produce meaningful descriptions of achievement, not to teach you any more statistics than you already know.

Measuring an individual student's growth. Measuring an individual student's growth is easiest when you have comparable data at two different times. Comparable data at two time points can be hard to come by. We have already seen that many state tests don't have vertical scales, so you can't compare a student's scale score on the 4th grade test with his scale score on the 5th grade test he took the following year.

You can compare percentile ranks from one assessment occasion to the next, but you are very limited in what you can say about the meaning of this comparison. For example, if Jordan was at the 32nd percentile on the 3rd grade mathematics test and at the 50th percentile on the 4th grade test, you can say that his place among his peers has shifted. He has moved from being more competent in mathematics (as measured by this test) than a third of his peers to being more competent than half of them. You need to make two big assumptions in order to say this. First, you need to assume that the norm group was relevant and appropriate, and comparable for each test. Second, you need to assume that the domain of "mathematics" measured by the 3rd grade test was comparable to the domain measured by the 4th grade test.

Some benchmark assessments are designed to produce comparable standardized test scores from one assessment occasion to the next during the same year. Changes in scale scores or percentile ranks over two or three benchmark tests can show growth within a school year. Even when you have comparable measures, however, remember that test scores are still *mental* measurements—estimates of what is inside a student's head. They are not oysters you can count so that you know exactly how many you have. There is a margin of error associated with estimating what's inside a student's head. Before you interpret the magnitude of changes, see if you can find out what the standard error of measurement (an estimate of that margin of error) is for the test scores you're looking at. Some assessments report standard errors on their score reports. For other assessments, you may need to ask the school psychologist or district assessment director to look in the assessment's technical manual. Any changes within that margin could be simply a result of chance.

Changes in performance categories (e.g., Proficient) from year to year, on a state test or any assessment, as we have seen, are more problematic to interpret than changes in scale scores or percentile ranks. However, this is often information that the student, his parents, and his teacher want to see. If you are going to look at changes in performance categories, make sure you interpret the change as the student moving past a cut score into another area of the distribution of student performance. Improving from Basic to Proficient means there was learning, sure, but it signifies little or nothing about *how much* learning. If a student was close to the cut score to begin with, he could have improved very little and still crossed the cut score on the next test.

To really know *what* students are learning, I recommend supplementing any of these large-scale descriptions of individual growth with a selection of student work in the relevant content area that shows the kinds of things the student is able to do with his knowledge and skills. If your educational decision targeted a manageable number of students, I recommend having them keep a *growth portfolio* (Brookhart & Nitko, 2015) that includes evidence of changes in their work over time in the particular area of interest and their reflections on the work and their learning.

Measuring growth of groups of students. Measuring growth of groups of students adds a level of complexity to your thinking because each "data point" is actually a summary of many data points—one for everyone in the group. So there is both a measure of central tendency (we usually use the mean or median, which are two different kinds of averages) and a measure of how spread out students' scores are. The range, the distance from the lowest to the highest scores, is often useful to know. Other measures of spread you may hear about are the *standard deviation* and the *interquartile range*. The standard deviation is a measure of how spread out scores are around the mean and is often used, for example, to describe a group's spread of scores around their mean scale score on a state test. The interquartile range, the distance between the 25th percentile and the 75th percentile, is a measure of the extent to which scores are spread out around the median, because the median is the 50th percentile.

We saw an example of comparing mean scale scores in the School 2 example in Chapter 2. The state test scores for School 2 were reported as both percentages of students in different proficiency categories and as mean scale scores. In that state, scale scores were not comparable from grade to grade, so we couldn't compare, say, 6th graders to 7th graders. But we could meaningfully compare the mean scale scores in mathematics for 6th graders over the last four years. A line graph worked well to show "growth" in 6th grade achievement from year to year. Always be sure to describe what you are comparing. In this case, it was "6th grade performance" that rose, not the achievement of any particular 6th graders, because each year's group of students was different.

Another way to compare performance from one occasion to the next on comparable tests is to compare median percentile ranks. Because percentile ranks don't have equal intervals—there is more distance between ranks at the low and high ends of the distribution than in the middle—you can't average them in a meaningful way. But you can line them up and find the middle, which is what the median does. If you are comparing percentile ranks for groups, use the median.

I hope you remember from Chapter 2 that comparing percentages in categories is *not* a meaningful way to describe change in learning, because this measure has a lot of volatility and, what's worse, that volatility is different depending on where the cut score is located in the distribution of test scores. However, sometimes there is an administrative or a political need to describe changes in *scoring*, as in, for example, a newspaper headline that says "Over 80% of Local 5th Graders Now Proficient in Reading," or something like that. Advising you not to do something you may end up having to do seems kind of lame. So my advice is: Don't do it! Don't report changes in percentages of students in proficiency categories. But if you *have* to, as before, *describe what you are comparing*. In this case you are comparing scoring patterns, not describing learning gains. The most you can say is, "Last year 74 percent of our students scored at the Proficient level or above in reading, and this year 81 percent of them scored at that level."

So far we have been talking about describing what happened to *average* performance, but you may also want to think about changes in the *spread* of performance. To illustrate this with a familiar scale, let's consider that we have measures on two versions of a test that measure exactly the same thing (I'll have more to say about that in a minute) at two points in time, and the scores are on the scale of 0 to 100 percent correct. Suppose the average score rose from a first-test average of 80 to a second-test average of 82. As a group, the students' scores didn't increase very much. However, suppose that the spread of scores for the first test had been from 5 to 90, and the spread of scores on the second test was from 60 to 95. Somebody learned something! Of course, you'd need to check individual scores to see that it was the low-scorers on the first test who learned and the others who didn't, but that's the most likely explanation. The point of this illustration is that when you have a group you can look at both average performance and the spread of performance.

Before we leave the topic of comparable tests, stop to consider a common unit design in which you give a pre-test to start and a post-test at the end to see what students learned. Those tests should be comparable, but they should not be the exact same test, with identical questions or tasks. The reason? You won't be able to tell if students increased in learning or just remembered what was on the test. A good way to make pre-tests and post-tests comparable for instructional purposes is to create a test blueprint and then build both tests to the same blueprint. That way, both tests will have the same type of questions, covering the same learning outcomes and levels of thinking, but will not confound "learning the test items" with learning in the domain assessed.

It is important to stress that when I talk about "comparability" in this manner I do not mean the same thing a psychometrician means when he says that tests are "equated." True equating requires both tests to satisfy rigorous statistical requirements (Linn, 1993). Other methods of linking scores exist for tests that don't quite meet these requirements, as well. When you are comparing teacher-made or other school-based tests, you are not, in fact, comparing equated tests. You are looking at estimates of performance in a domain on two different tests. For the purpose of evaluating local instructional changes, however, the fidelity of the classroom test to exactly what was taught in the classroom is valuable, and there may be no standardized measure of exactly what you have taught. So think of your comparisons as estimates of differences, not precise measures of them.

Finally, as I mentioned in Chapter 2, there are many more complex ways to calculate student growth than looking at simple change over time. These are usually either a set of decision rules, such as ascribing a point for every student who moves up one category level (e.g., from Proficient to Advanced), or a statistical model comparing scores and sometimes controlling for other variables. I don't recommend using these for internal evaluation studies of the effects of educational decisions.

Being cautious about describing cause and change

When you use a logic model, make a change, and then measure its "effectiveness" by figuring out how well your intended outcomes materialized, it is really easy to fall into the trap of concluding that your educational decision—your instructional change or whatever it was—is the *cause* of increased learning. How a logic model works for evaluating decisions is more like how we teach students to write and think, or how a lawyer makes a case, than an experimental design that can show cause. When students write, as you know, we say, "State your conclusion and support it with logic and evidence." We don't say, "Prove it beyond a shadow of a doubt." Or when a lawyer makes a case, she convinces people that her explanation of the crime is the most likely and is beyond reasonable doubt, not that she has an ironclad "proof." (If you doubt that, consider all the news stories about wrongly convicted prisoners who are vindicated years after their trials.)

A logic model is an evaluation tool that allows you to plan an educational decision and to identify, collect, and organize evidence you want to look at about what happened. Your evaluation is a judgment of whether what happened after the change was useful or valuable and whether it was what you intended. You can build up evidence to make your case. For example, you might see improvements in students' classroom work and also talk with teachers who might say, for example, that when they taught their first lessons on author's purpose, students seemed very unfamiliar with the idea, but as the year progressed, students really enjoyed becoming "text detectives." Thus you support your hypothesis that adding more depth to the reading curriculum will be associated with these important results.

Why is this important? Because to demonstrate that one thing *caused* another, you need an experimental design in which everything except that one thing is held constant. You simply can't do that in live school. You have different students and teachers from one year to the next. Some work harder than others. Some have different readiness for learning than others. You have different resources (maybe new computers). You have different weather (witness how school closings during years with harsh winters change instruction). Current events and school events are different from year to year. I could go on, but you get the point. There is no such thing as a controlled experiment for one educational decision within the context of a real classroom, school, or district. Sometimes you can get close, but that's all you can hope for.

This isn't a problem unless you misrepresent your logic model as a proof of cause. Simply say that your evaluation results suggested that the data-based decision you made, whatever it was, had good outcomes for these students, who did these things, this year. Make your case for probable cause. Use the logic from your model and multiple sources of evidence. It's better to have a high-quality evaluation, with arguments and evidence, than a flawed experiment. Then turn right around and, using the data from your evaluation, query it, ask your questions, develop your tentative hypothesis, plan your next improvement and the evidence you will seek, and get on with the next cycle of data-based decision making.

Next, let's finish up the examples of School 1 and School 2. Then we'll consider some other evaluations of student learning after educational decisions.

Example—School 1

School 1, you will remember, had decided that the problem was that the current reading curriculum centered too narrowly on literal and inferential comprehension and did not include other aspects of the state reading standards. During some summer work time, the reading teachers met and modified the curriculum. They included learning goals about analyzing author's purpose and intended audience and comparing texts. They brainstormed some ways they might do that in the classroom—for example, having students compare and contrast the author's depiction of a future society in

The Hunger Games by Suzanne Collins with the society depicted in *The Giver* by Lois Lowry and the ways in which each influenced the plot, characters, and themes of the respective novels.

During the year, they taught these new lessons along with lessons on comprehension, modifying their instructional planning to match the curriculum modifications they had made. To find out how students were thinking about text, they looked at classroom assignments where students had to analyze texts deeply. They also looked at classroom measures of comprehension, because they didn't want their changes to result in the diminishment of students' reading comprehension. To find out about students' attitudes and interests, each teacher also conducted, in her own classes, 10-minute class discussions after one of the new assignments was finished. In one of their data meetings, teachers reported what students had said, and a recorder took notes. All these classroom-based measures and observations were part of the next-to-last box in the logic model School 1 was using. Their thinking was that the immediate results of instruction would show more clearly in observations closer to the learning.

This turned out to be a good strategy, because the following year's state test scores in reading (the last box in their logic model) improved, but not by a huge amount. The percentage of Advanced and Proficient students each increased by 5 percent. Given the volatility of changes in percentages, without the classroom data showing what kinds of literary analyses students could now do, they would have been hard pressed to declare their curricular and instructional modifications had led to desired outcomes.

The classroom data also became the foundation for School 1's subsequent data-based decision about teaching reading. The classroom work—both the scores and the work itself—contained information on which students and what kind of literary analyses seemed most problematic. The reading teachers decided to use that information to identify a problem and a potential solution that might help them teach literary analysis more successfully to lower-achievers. Specifically, they decided that the modified curriculum should stay as is. What they decided to change was involving students more intentionally in seeking to understand daily learning targets and criteria for success (student look-fors), as well as the larger learning goals. Their next logic model set forth the expectation that clarifying what the various approaches to text looked like would help all students, and lower-achievers especially.

Example—School 2

School 2 had decided to work on instructional changes, emphasizing more problem identification and mathematical thinking and less rote application of predetermined procedures. The math teachers in School 2 participated in some professional development in order to enlarge their repertoire of teaching strategies, instructional activities, and assessments in mathematics to include more higher-order thinking and quantitative reasoning.

As in School 1, the first kind of evidence they looked at was student classroom work. To do this, they adopted a math problem-solving rubric that evaluated the problem solving separately from the mathematical computation. Teachers used this rubric with students, helping them chart their own progress. Students did weekly problems that were not routine, related to the math content in their units but requiring previously learned content and more than one step to solve. Students conferenced with each other and the teacher on these weekly formative assessment opportunities.

School 2's logic model, like School 1's, specified a look at classroom assessments in the next-to-last box in the model. The math teachers looked at student performance on these nonroutine problems; using the rubric, they could evaluate problem-solving and computational skills separately. They also observed the quality of students' peer and self-evaluations, which students had recorded on copies of the rubric.

In general, teachers were pleased with students' problem solving and mathematical thinking. The state test scores bore this out, rising an average of 10 scale-score points per grade, even for the previously stagnant 8th grade scores. Based on these data, School 2 decided to continue its emphasis on mathematical thinking. The teachers decided that during the next year, they would investigate the possibility of two enhancements to their mathematics instruction. They decided to continue their professional development to increase teachers' repertoire of ways to teach and assess mathematical thinking even further. They also decided to work with teachers in other disci-plines (for example, in science and social studies classes) to see if they could embed some mathematical problem solving into other content areas.

Data-Based Decision Making Writ Small (but Mighty!): Students Charting Their Own Growth

I'd like to add to the set of examples in this chapter by making the case that teachers aren't the only ones who can and should do data-based decision mak-ing. Having students keep track of their own work is a tried-and-true way to involve students in their own data and, in the process, in their own learning. I have used the example of Minute Math before (Moss & Brookhart, 2009). It's the clearest example I have to show, and we have established that it improved both learning and motivation (Brookhart, Andolina, Zuza, & Furman, 2004), which is an important argument for involving students in data-based decision making.

Third graders were learning their basic math facts, one fact-family per quarter. First, they learned addition facts to 10, then subtraction, multiplica-tion, and division. During the time they were learning multiplication, I was supervising a student teacher who decided she would try helping her students with goal setting, metacognition, planning, and studying—in short, all kinds of higher-order skills that were not present in the rote memorization of tables of math facts. The tool she devised for doing this was a student version of data-based decision making. The other 3rd grade class used the process, as well.

The nature of the data was simple enough that even 3rd graders under-stood it. Every week, they took a 100-fact timed test to see how many facts they could get correct in five minutes. For our purposes in this book (we didn't explain this to the 3rd graders), it's worth noting that the data were percent-correct scores, so they were able to be graphed on an equal-interval axis. The test was the same each week, so the scores were comparable, meaning a graph of progress over time would be interpretable.

Students predicted the score they thought they would achieve on the next test, then graphed it. The following Friday, they took their test and graphed their real performance, then predicted the following Friday's score. At that point, students filled in a goal sheet that required them to say what their *learning* goal was (e.g., "to learn my 8 tables better") and a plan for achieving that goal, as well as their scoring goal. Actually, one class did a better job at stressing that the goal had to be about learning as well as scoring, and that turned out to make a difference in both learning and motivation (Brookhart et al., 2004), but for this description we'll just stick with the one class, where my student teacher and her cooperating teacher used this process skillfully.

Most of the students showed over-prediction for the first week, followed by remarkably accurate predictions and climbing up their "steps," as they called the increasing bars in their bar graphs. Most reached a score of 100 percent or nearly so by the end of the 10 weeks. But there were also quite a few who topped out in the middle of the project but were having so much fun they didn't want to stop. Jason, whose graph appears in Figure 7.1, had learned his times tables by the fifth week. If you look closely at weeks 6 through 10, you can see that Jason challenged himself to do the multiplication facts test in four minutes, and then three minutes.

Why is this data-based decision making? Because each week after their prediction, students were required by the goal sheets to set a learning goal and make a plan—a decision about what to do—to reach the goal. Some of the common action plans included using flash cards, going over the facts at home with parents or siblings, and studying using a times-table chart. Each week the students checked their data and decided whether to continue their plan or change it for the next week. They used their data to evaluate the effectiveness of their previous studying decisions and to make a new decision about studying for the following week.

Concluding Thoughts

Data-based decision making is a cycle. An important part of that cycle is evaluating whether the decision you made took instruction and learning in the direction you intended it to go. That means, of course, more data. This chapter has presented and illustrated several different ways to evaluate decisions

FIGURE 7.1

Prediction and Record Sheet for Basic Multiplication Timed Tasks

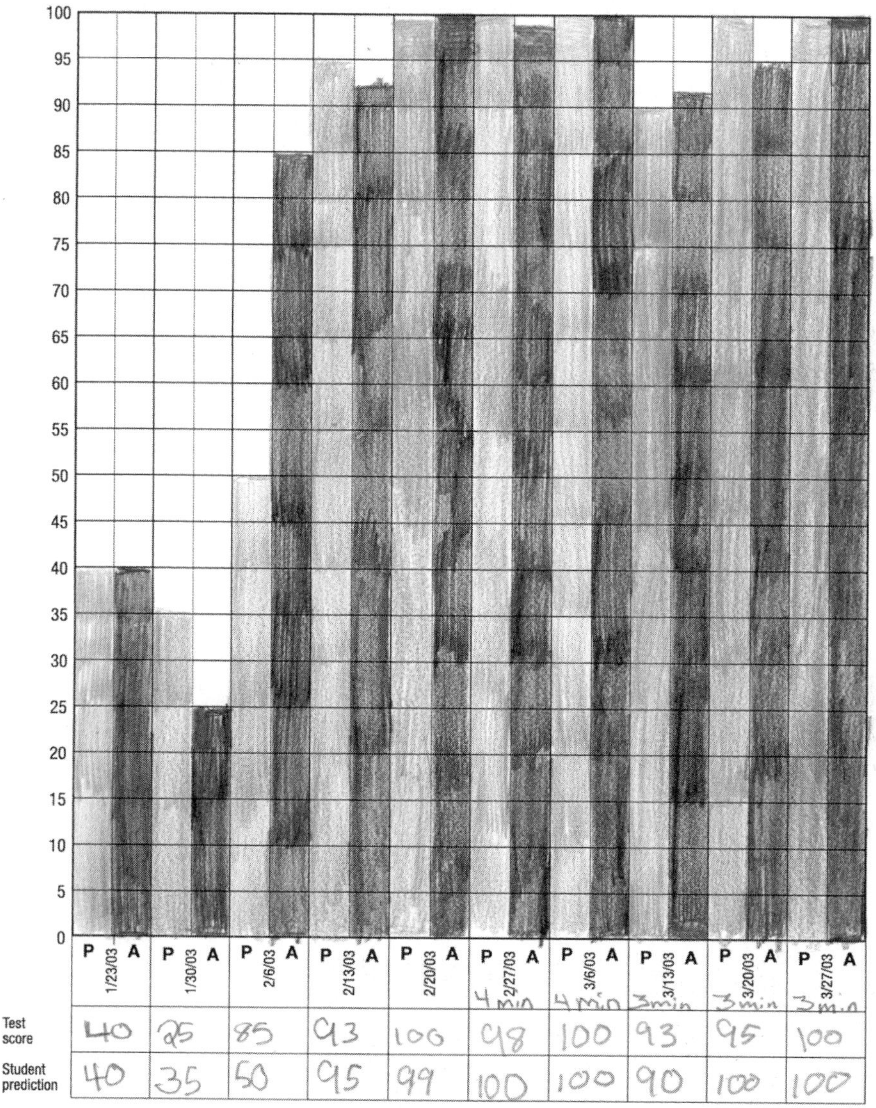

	1/23/03	1/30/03	2/6/03	2/13/03	2/20/03	2/27/03 4 min	3/6/03 4 min	3/13/03 3 min	3/20/03 3 min	3/27/03 3 min
Test score	40	25	85	93	100	98	100	93	95	100
Student prediction	40	35	50	95	99	100	100	90	100	100

Name Jason

P = Predicted score (light gray)
A = Actual score (medium gray)

about curriculum and instruction made by teachers and decisions about studying made by students.

Looking at evaluation data should follow the same principles as were laid out in Chapters 2 through 5 for treating different kinds of data. Determine what kind of data you need for your evaluation, using your logic model. Analyze the data appropriately, according to the type of information you have. Then make some conclusions and enter the next cycle of data-based decision making. I sum up this process and the usefulness of the four-quadrant framework in the final chapter.

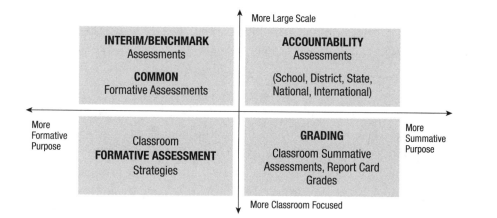

This book has presented two major tools for maintaining a balanced assessment system and using data routinely in order to monitor and improve teaching and learning. The first is the four-quadrant framework for thinking about data related to student learning. A major point was that there are different kinds of data, depending on both the purpose and scope of the measures and on the type of scores they produce. You have to know what kind of data you have—in both senses—in order to interpret results meaningfully. The second tool is the data-based decision-making process, which is a relative of the action research process.

What's "Different" About Different Kinds of Data?

The theme of "different kinds of data" is almost a play on words, because data are different in several senses. We've used the four-quadrant framework to show how data differ in purpose (formative or summative) and focus (classroom or large-scale). We've explored how those differences lead to differences in the construct that's being measured, from a very coarse-grained summary of a whole domain such as "reading" to fine-grained information about specific knowledge and skills. Differences in purpose and focus also lead to differences in who is measured, what kinds of distributions of performance are expected, and how results are reported.

Another big idea has been the type of scale used in an assessment—or, in the case of classroom formative assessment, the lack of a scale. Some assessment results, such as scale scores and percent-correct scores, are on a scale on which each point is the same distance from all other points. For these numbers, you can calculate means and standard deviations. Some numbers, including percentile ranks, letter grades, and proficiency categories, are ordered categories. The categories encompass different "amounts" of learning, and the amount of progress is not the same from one category to the next. For these categories, you can calculate medians and interquartile ranges, but you can't, for example, determine an "average" percentile rank. Classroom formative assessment results come in the form of teacher feedback, student insights about where they are in their learning, and decisions about next steps, and the results do not form a scale. You typically don't aggregate these results, but rather help your students act on them individually.

As we discussed types of numbers and what you can and can't meaningfully do with the different types of scales, we also looked at some issues that occur when you try to interpret numbers. Probably the most dramatic of these was the problem of using cut scores to create ordered categories (e.g., Advanced, Proficient, Not Proficient) out of an underlying continuous distribution of scale scores, showing how the resulting percentages in those categories can be a misleading and dangerous metric. Another issue we looked at was the fact that a typical grade distribution is negatively skewed, meaning that typically most of the students learn most of what they're supposed to learn.

We also looked at types of comparisons, showing that a comparison in the same grade across years means there are different students in each group. A comparison of the same students across years means there are different tests at each time point. A comparison across grades in the same year means there are different students and different tests at each point. Any of these can be reasonable things to do as long as you know what you're comparing and can explain the comparison properly.

Data-Based Decision Making

Equipped with a clear understanding of data, you can begin the data-based decision-making process. Start with data, but use them to question. The data do not constitute a problem; they are just a symptom or an indicator. Data need to be interpreted, and then further data need to be collected in order to formulate a tentative explanation or hypothesis about what is going on—what problem you want to solve. Once you have tentatively identified the problem, try out a solution and evaluate it—with more data. Then start the cycle again.

Data-based decision making does not usually lead to "reports" in the sense of a white paper. However, results should be documented. Minutes or notes from meetings of a data team or a professional learning group, graphs made to highlight comparisons in data, logic models, and assessment results should be gathered and available for ongoing use. Just talking about data isn't enough. Record keeping is important.

Some smaller themes explored in the book are worth summarizing here, as well. Routine collection and review of data in a balanced assessment system was one of them. Any successful system needs good information to keep all its components interacting and functioning well. Looking at data should be business as usual in any system.

Another theme has been to keep the focus on learning. I have focused almost exclusively on assessments of student learning, not the wider world of data (which might include such elements as attendance and discipline), in keeping with the purpose of the book. A corollary to the focus on learning has been a focus on students. It is important to remember that behind every measure of student achievement is the student who is achieving—or not. Put a face, or groups of faces, on those numbers. Ask the students to help you monitor their learning. Give them strategies and tools to do that. Ultimately, of course, it *is* their learning.

Glossary

If a term has multiple meanings, this glossary defines the term as it is used in this book.

bar graph—A presentation of data using the height of a bar to represent a value; especially suited to graphing data reported in ordered categories.

benchmark assessment—An assessment that allows interpretations of student performance against standards.

classroom-based—Grounded in classroom instruction and assessment; used to describe interventions, data, and observations.

classroom formative assessment—Assessment carried out for the purpose of informing students' and teachers' next steps in classroom instruction and learning.

common formative assessment—An assessment given for the purpose of informing instructional decisions across classrooms.

criterion-referenced—Interpreted according to explicit standards or a description of what students scoring at a certain level know and can do; used to interpret a student's performance.

cut score—A score designated as the boundary between two categories, for example, between Proficient and Not Proficient.

formative—For the purpose of contributing to learning.

grading—Assessment carried out at the classroom level for the purpose of summarizing and reporting achievement.

growth model—A set of decision rules or a statistical model that describes changes in student achievement from one occasion to another.

interim assessment—An assessment of student achievement against standards, carried out across classrooms, for the purpose of informing changes in instruction.

interquartile range—The distance between the 25th percentile and the 75th percentile, or "the distance between the quartiles."

large-scale assessment—An assessment that is administered and interpreted across more than one classroom.

line graph—A presentation of data as a series of points connected with a line; especially suited to graphing equal-interval data.

logic model—A graphical depiction of the relationships between causes and effects, used for evaluation.

mean—The arithmetic average of scores; a measure of central tendency arrived at by summing the scores in a distribution and dividing by the number of scores.

median—A measure of central tendency that separates the lower and upper halves of scores in a distribution; also known as the 50th percentile.

mental measurement—A measure of an internal construct, usually a cognitive or an affective construct such as achievement, attitudes, or interests, relative to a particular domain.

norm group—The reference group against which norm-referenced scores are interpreted.

norm-referenced—Interpreted by comparing a student's performance with that of other students.

percent (percentage)—A ratio or proportion expressed as a fraction of 100.

percentile rank—The percentage of scores that are the same or lower than a given score in a distribution.

range—The distance between the highest and lowest scores in a distribution; a measure of the spread of scores.

scale score—A score on an arbitrary scale, to which a raw score has been converted by considering additional information.

self-referenced—Interpreted by comparing a student's performance with his own previous or expected performance.

standard deviation—A measure of the spread of scores around the mean.

standardized test—A test that is administered and scored in the same manner for all test-takers, such that scores can be compared from one administration to another.

standards-referenced—Interpreted by comparing a student's score to where it falls in a distribution marked off by cut scores for performance categories (e.g., Proficient).

summative—For the purpose of certifying or reporting learning.

test blueprint (also called *table of specifications*)—A diagram or chart describing the content of a test according to what learning outcomes are assessed at what cognitive level(s).

vertical scale score—A score on a scale that extends upward and downward across different grade levels, useful for comparing students' performance across grade levels.

References

Abrams, L. M., & McMillan, J. H. (2013). The instructional influence of interim assessments: Voices from the field. In R. W. Lissitz (Ed.), *Informing the practice of teaching using formative and interim assessment* (pp. 105–133). Charlotte, NC: Information Age Publishing.

Andrade, H. L. (2010). Students as the definitive source of formative assessment: Academic self-assessment and self-regulation of learning. In H. L. Andrade & G. J. Cizek (Eds.), *Handbook of formative assessment* (pp. 90–105). New York: Routledge.

Atkinson, R. C., & Geiser, S. (2009). Reflections on a century of college admissions tests. *Educational Researcher, 38*(9), 665–676.

Au, W. (2007). High-stakes testing and curricular control: A qualitative metasynthesis. *Educational Researcher, 36*(5), 258–267.

Bandeira de Mello, V., Blankenship, C., & McLaughlin, D. H. (2009). *Mapping state proficiency standards onto NAEP scales: 2005–2007* (NCES 2010-456). National Center for Education Statistics, Institute of Education Sciences, U.S. Department of Education. Washington, DC.

Baum, M. H. (2011). *Using short-cycle interim assessment to improve educator evaluation, educator effectiveness, and student achievement.* Wisconsin Rapids, WI: Renaissance Learning.

Black, P., & Wiliam, D. (1998). Assessment and classroom learning. *Assessment in Education, 5*(1), 7–74.

Black, P. J., & Wiliam, D. (2009). Developing the theory of formative assessment. *Educational Assessment, Evaluation, and Accountability, 21*(1), 5–31.

Blanc, S., Christman, J. B., Liu, R., Mitchell, C., Travers, E., & Bulkley, K. (2010). Learning to learn from data: Benchmarks and instructional communities. *Peabody Journal of Education, 85*(2), 205–225.

Boudett, K. P., City, E. A., & Murnane, R. J. (Eds.). (2013). *Data wise: A step-by-step guide to using assessment results to improve teaching and learning* (2nd ed.). Cambridge, MA: Harvard Education Press.

Bowers, A. J. (2010). Analyzing the longitudinal K–12 grading histories of entire cohorts of students: Grades, data driven decision making, dropping out and hierarchical cluster analysis. *Practical Assessment, Research & Evaluation, 15*(7). Available: http://pareonline.net/getvn.asp?v=15&n=7

Bowers, A. J., & Sprott, R. (2012). Examining the multiple trajectories associated with dropping out of high school: A growth mixture model analysis. *Journal of Educational Research, 105*(3), 176–195.

Bowers, A. J., Sprott, R., & Taff, S. A. (2013). Do we know who will drop out? A review of the predictors of dropping out of high school: Precision, sensitivity and specificity. *The High School Journal, 96*(2), 77–100.

Brookhart, S. M. (2001). Successful students' formative and summative uses of assessment information. *Assessment in Education, 8*(2), 153–169.

Brookhart, S. M. (2007). Expanding views about formative classroom assessment: A review of the literature. In J. H. McMillan (Ed.), *Formative classroom assessment: Theory into practice* (pp. 43–62). New York: Teachers College Press.

Brookhart, S. M. (2011). *Grading and learning: Practices that support student achievement.* Bloomington, IN: Solution Tree.

Brookhart, S. M. (2013). Comprehensive assessment systems in service of learning: Getting the balance right. In R. W. Lissitz (Ed.), *Informing the practice of teaching using formative and interim assessment: A systems approach* (pp. 165–184). Charlotte, NC: Information Age Publishing.

Brookhart, S. M. (in press). Graded achievement, tested achievement, and validity. *Educational Assessment.*

Brookhart, S. M., Andolina, M., Zuza, M., & Furman, R. (2004). Minute math: An action research study of student self-assessment. *Educational Studies in Mathematics, 57*(2), 213–227.

Brookhart, S. M., & Nitko, A. J. (2015). *Educational assessment of students* (7th ed.). Boston: Pearson.

Brown, R. S., & Coughlin, E. (2007, November). *The predictive validity of selected benchmark assessments used in the Mid-Atlantic Region* (Issues & Answers Report, REL 2007–No. 017). Washington, DC: U.S. Department of Education, Institute of Education Sciences, National Center for Education Evaluation and Regional Assistance, Regional Educational Laboratory Mid-Atlantic.

Castellano, K. E., & Ho, A. D. (2013, February). *A practitioner's guide to growth models.* Council of Chief State School Officers. Retrieved February 23, 2015, from http://www.ccsso.org/Resources/Publications/A_Practitioners_Guide_to_Growth_Models.html

Cizek, G. J. (Ed.). (2001). *Setting performance standards: Concepts, methods, and perspectives.* Mahwah, NJ: Lawrence Erlbaum Associates.

Crane, E. (2010). *Building an interim assessment system: A workbook for school districts.* Washington, DC: Council of Chief State School Officers.

Datnow, A., & Hubbard, L. (2015). Teachers' use of assessment data to inform instruction. *Teachers College Record, 117*(4), 1–26.

Gallimore, R., Ermeling, B. A., Saunders, W. M., & Goldenberg, C. (2009). Moving the learning of teaching closer to practice: Teacher education implications of school-based inquiry teams. *Elementary School Journal, 109*(5), 537–553.

Goertz, M. E., Oláh, L. N., & Riggan, M. (2009). *From testing to teaching: The use of interim assessments in classroom instruction.* Consortium for Policy Research in Education Research Report # RR-65.

Hamilton, L., Halverson, R., Jackson, S. S., Mandinach, E., Supovitz, J. A., & Wayman, J. C. (2009). *Using student achievement data to support instructional decision making* (NCEE 2009-4067). Washington, DC: National Center for Education Evaluation and Regional Assistance, Institute of Education Sciences, U.S. Department of Education. Retrieved from http://ies.ed.gov/ncee/wwc/PracticeGuide.aspx?sid=12

Hattie, J., & Timperley, H. (2007). The power of feedback. *Review of Educational Research, 77*(1), 81–112.

Heritage, M. (2010). *Formative assessment: Making it happen in the classroom.* Thousand Oaks, CA: Sage.

Ho, A. D. (2008). The problem with "proficiency": Limitations of statistics and policy under No Child Left Behind. *Educational Researcher, 37*(6), 351–360.

Huff, K., Steinberg, L., & Matts, T. (2010). The promises and challenges of implementing evidence-centered design in large-scale assessment. *Applied Measurement in Education, 23*(4), 310–324.

Illinois State Board of Education (ISBE). (2013, February). *Guidebook on student learning objectives for Type III assessments.* Illinois State Board of Education Performance Evaluation Advisory Council.

James-Ward, C., Fisher, D., Frey, N., & Lapp, D. (2013). *Using data to focus instructional improvement.* Alexandria, VA: ASCD.

Kingston, N., & Nash, B. (2011). Formative assessment: A meta-analysis and a call for research. *Educational Measurement: Issues and Practice, 30*(4), 28–37.

Koch, M. J., & DeLuca, C. (2012). Rethinking validation in complex high-stakes assessment contexts. *Assessment in Education: Principles, Policy & Practice, 19*(1), 99–116.

Konstantopoulos, S., Miller, S., van der Ploeg, A., Li, C.-H., & Traynor, A. (2011, September). *The impact of Indiana's system of diagnostic assessments on mathematics achievement.* Paper presented at the Fall 2011 Conference of the Society for Research on Educational Effectiveness, Washington, DC.

Leahy, S., Lyon, C., Thompson, M., & Wiliam, D. (2005, November). Classroom assessment: Minute by minute, day by day. *Educational Leadership, 63*(3), 19–24.

Linn, R. L. (1993). Linking results of distinct assessments. *Applied Measurement in Education, 6*(1), 83–102.

McIntosh, S. (2012, September). *State high school exit exams: A policy in transition.* Washington, DC: Center on Education Policy.

Miami-Dade County Public Schools. (2008, October). How interim assessments affect student achievement. *Information Capsule: Research Services,* vol. 0804. Available: http://drs.dadeschools.net/InformationCapsules/IC0804.PDF

Moss, C. M. (2013). Research on classroom summative assessment. In J. H. McMillan (Ed.), *Handbook of research on classroom assessment* (pp. 235–255). Los Angeles: Sage.

Moss, C. M., & Brookhart, S. M. (2009). *Advancing formative assessment in every classroom: A guide for instructional leaders.* Alexandria, VA: ASCD.

New York State Education Department (NYSED). (2014, March). *Guidance on the New York State district-wide growth goal-setting process for teachers: Student learning objectives.* Author.

No Child Left Behind Act of 2001. (2002). Pub. L. No. 107–110, 115 Stat. 1425.

Noffke, S. E., & Somekh, B. (Eds.). (2009). *The SAGE handbook of educational action research.* London: SAGE.

Northwest Evaluation Association (NWEA). (2012, January). *RIT Scale Norms Study: For use with Northwest Evaluation Association Measures of Academic Progress® (MAP®) and MAP for Primary Grades.* Portland, OR: Author.

PARCC. (2013, February). *PARCC college- and career-ready determination policy in English language arts/literacy and mathematics & policy-level performance level descriptors.* Adopted by the PARCC Governing Board and Advisory Committee on College Readiness, October 25, 2012, revised February 20, 2013. Retrieved February 23, 2015, from http://www.parcconline.org/CCRD

Pattison, E., Grodsky, E., & Muller, C. (2013). Is the sky falling? Grade inflation and the signaling power of grades. *Educational Researcher, 42*(5), 259–265.

Perie, M., Marion, S., & Gong, B. (2009). Moving toward a comprehensive assessment system: A framework for considering interim assessments. *Educational Measurement: Issues and Practice, 28*(3), 5–13.

Perie, M., Park, J., & Klau, K. (2007, December). *Key elements for educational accountability models.* Washington, DC: Council of Chief State School Officers.

Riggan, M., & Oláh, L. N. (2011). Locating interim assessments within teachers' assessment practice. *Educational Assessment, 16*(1), 1–14.

Ross, J. A., Hogaboam-Gray, A., & Rolheiser, C. (2002). Student self-evaluation in grade 5–6 mathematics: Effects on problem-solving achievement. *Educational Assessment, 8*(1), 43–58.

Sadler, D. R. (1989). Formative assessment and the design of instructional systems. *Instructional Science, 18*(2), 119–144.

Saunders, W. M., Goldenberg, C. N., & Gallimore, R. (2009). Increasing achievement by focusing grade-level teams on improving classroom learning: A prospective, quasi-experimental study of Title 1 schools. *American Educational Research Journal, 46*(4), 1006–1033.

Sawyer, R. (2013). Beyond correlations: Usefulness of high school GPA and test scores in making college admissions decisions. *Applied Measurement in Education, 26,* 89–112.

Shepard, L. A. (2000). The role of assessment in a learning culture. *Educational Researcher, 29*(7), 4–14.

Shepard, L. A. (2006). Classroom assessment. In R. L. Brennan (Ed.), *Educational measurement* (4th ed., pp. 623–646). Westport, CT: Praeger.

Sloan, W. M. (2012, July). What is the purpose of education? *Education Update, 54*(7).

Smarter Balanced Assessment Consortium. (2013a, April). *Initial achievement level descriptors and college content-readiness policy: ELA.* Retrieved February 23, 2015, from http://www.smarterbalanced.org/achievement-levels/

Smarter Balanced Assessment Consortium. (2013b, April). *Initial achievement level descriptors and college content-readiness policy: Mathematics.* Retrieved February 23, 2015, from http://www.smarterbalanced.org/achievement-levels/

Smarter Balanced Assessment Consortium. (2014, February). *Appendix B: Grade level tables for all claims and assessment targets and item types.* Retrieved January 9, 2015, from http://www.smarterbalanced.org/wordpress/wp-content/uploads/2011/12/ELA-Literacy-Content-Specifications.pdf

Third International Conference on Assessment for Learning. (2009). Position paper on assessment for learning from the Third International Conference on Assessment for Learning, Dunedin, New Zealand. *Educational Measurement: Issues and Practice, 28*(3), 3–4.

Thorsen, C., & Cliffordson, C. (2012). Teachers' grade assignment and the predictive validity of criterion-referenced grades. *Educational Research and Evaluation, 18*(2), 153–172.

Waltman, K. K., & Frisbie, D. A. (1994). Parents' understanding of their children's report card grades. *Applied Measurement in Education, 7*(3), 223–240.

Wiliam, D. (2010). An integrative summary of the research literature and implications for a new theory of formative assessment. In H. L. Andrade & G. J. Cizek (Eds.), *Handbook of Formative Assessment* (pp. 18–40). New York: Routledge.

Wiliam, D. (2011). *Embedded formative assessment.* Bloomington, IN: Solution Tree.

Index

Note: The letter *f* following a page number denotes a figure. The letter *g* denotes a definition in the glossary.

About the Author

Susan M. Brookhart, PhD, is an independent educational consultant based in Helena, Montana. She has taught both elementary and middle school. She was professor and chair of the Department of Educational Foundations and Leadership at Duquesne University, where she currently serves as an adjunct professor. She has been the education columnist for *National Forum*, the journal of Phi Kappa Phi, and editor of *Educational Measurement: Issues and Practice*, a journal of the National Council on Measurement in Education. She is the author or coauthor of several books, including ASCD's *How to Give Effective Feedback to Your Students* and *How to Create and Use Rubrics for Formative Assessment and Grading*. She is the coauthor, with Connie M. Moss, of ASCD's *Advancing Formative Assessment in Every Classroom: A Guide for Instructional Leaders; Formative Classroom Walkthroughs: How Principals and Teachers Collaborate to Raise Student Achievement;* and *Learning Targets: Helping Students Aim for Understanding in Today's Lesson.* She was named the 2014 Jason Millman Scholar by the Consortium for Research on Educational Effectiveness and Teaching Effectiveness (CREATE) and received the 2015 Samuel J. Messick Lecture Award from ETS/TOEFL. She may be reached at susanbrookhart@bresnan.net.

Related ASCD Resources: Student Assessment and Data

At the time of publication, the following ASCD resources were available (ASCD stock numbers appear in parentheses). For up-to-date information about ASCD resources, go to www.ascd.org.

ASCD EDge® Group

Exchange ideas and connect with other educators interested in assessment on the social networking site ASCD EDge at http://ascdedge.ascd.org/

Print Products

Advancing Formative Assessment in Every Classroom: A Guide for Instructional Leaders by Connie M. Moss and Susan M. Brookhart (#109031)

Assessment and Student Success in a Differentiated Classroom by Carol Ann Tomlinson and Tonya R. Moon (#108028)

Checking for Understanding: Formative Assessment Techniques for Your Classroom, 2nd edition by Douglas Fisher and Nancy Frey (#115011)

Formative Assessment Strategies for Every Classroom: An ASCD Action Tool, 2nd edition by Susan M. Brookhart (#111005)

How Teachers Can Turn Data into Action by Daniel R. Venables (#114007)

Test Better, Teach Better: The Instructional Role of Assessment by W. James Popham (#102088)

Transformative Assessment by W. James Popham (#108018)

Transformative Assessment in Action: An Inside Look at Applying the Process by W. James Popham (#111008)

Using Data to Focus Instructional Improvement by Cheryl James-Ward, Douglas Fisher, Nancy Frey, and Diane Lapp (#113003)

What Teachers Really Need to Know About Formative Assessment by Laura Greenstein (#110017)

THE WHOLE CHILD The Whole Child Initiative helps schools and communities create learning environments that allow students to be healthy, safe, engaged, supported, and challenged. To learn more about other books and resources that relate to the whole child, visit www.wholechildeducation.org.

For more information: send e-mail to member@ascd.org; call 1-800-933-2723 or 703-578-9600, press 2; send a fax to 703-575-5400; or write to Information Services, ASCD, 1703 N. Beauregard St., Alexandria, VA 22311-1714 USA.